Panama

A Country Guide

Panama
A Country Guide

Tom Barry

The Inter-Hemispheric Education Resource Center

Albuquerque, New Mexico

Published by The Inter-Hemispheric Education Resource Center

ISBN: 0-911213-24-4

Library of Congress Catalog Card Number: 90-80321

The Inter-Hemispheric Education Resource Center
Box 4506 * Albuquerque, New Mexico * 87196

Acknowledgments

Without the assistance and encouragement of the Resource Center staff, this book on Panama would not have been possible. Research help was provided by Jenny Beatty, Joan MacLean, Felipe Montoya, Debra Preusch, and Thomas Weiss. In addition, Debra Preusch assisted with interviews and logistics, Connie Adler with editing, and Jenny Beatty with proofreading, wordprocessing, and production skills. I want to thank Charlotte Elton, Richard Millet, George Priestley, and John Weeks for commenting on the manuscript.

Table of Contents

The Resource Center

The Inter-Hemispheric Education Resource Center is a private non-profit research and policy institute located in Albuquerque, New Mexico. Founded in 1979, the Resource Center produces books, policy reports, and audiovisuals about U.S. foreign relations with third world countries. Among its most popular materials are *The Central America Fact Book* and the quarterly *Bulletin* mailed to subscribers for $5 annually ($7.50 outside the United States). For a catalogue of publications, please write to: The Resource Center, Box 4506, Albuquerque, NM 87196.

Panama

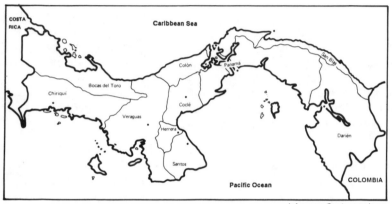

Inforpress Centroamericana

Introduction

Panama, the southernmost country in the Central American isthmus, stands apart from its neighbors. Although geographically it is clearly a Central American nation, Panama has not been included in regional bodies like the Central American Common Market. Neither has it been considered a South American nation even though it once was a province of Colombia.

It shares with most of its Central American neighbors a history bloodied by U.S. military intervention and is shaped by two U.S. enclaves: the banana plantations of United Fruit and the U.S. Canal Zone. No other country in the region, however, has been so thoroughly dominated by the United States — so much so that it has often taken the character of a U.S. protectorate. But even more than this close relationship with the United States, Panama's special and isolated character comes from its role as an international crossroads.

Panama was a territory of transit long before the Panama Canal was finished in 1914. King Charles V of Spain dreamed in 1534 of cutting a canal across Panama not long after the Spanish colonized this tropical land. Portobelo on the Caribbean coast was one of the major trading centers of the New World. In the 19th century the U.S.-built railroad took the forty-niners across the isthmus on their way to the hills of gold in California. Unlike elsewhere in Central America, the Panamanian elite were not a landed oligarchy but a business sector tied to international trade and services.

Panama, about the size of South Carolina, stands out as the country in the region with the highest per capita income, highest foreign investment, and most highly developed economic infrastructure. Over 90 percent of its 2.3 million inhabitants are literate and have access to potable water.

It is, however, a country of extreme contrasts. The shimmering office buildings and banks of Panama City face squalid slums. Looking out from the penthouse of these skyscrapers you can also see where the concrete and electric wires stop and the dense tropical forests begin. Over 40 percent of country's population live in the Panama City-Colón corridor that parallels the canal. Reaching southeast toward South America is a long strip of rainforest and swamps known as the Darién Gap. Like most of the country's Caribbean seaboard, except the city of Colón and United Fruit's banana plantations in the Bocas del Toro region, the Darién Gap is largely roadless and sparsely inhabited, though becoming rapidly deforested and colonized.

There are those who say that the name Panama comes from an Indian word meaning "land of many fish," while others insist that it stems from the Indian phrase *"panna mai."* When Spanish soldiers asked the Indians where they could find gold, they replied with that phrase meaning "far away."[1] Located in the humid torrid zone, Panama has a uniformly hot and humid climate, somewhat relieved at night by cool sea air. The rainy season runs from April to November, although no month is entirely free of rain. Over 500 waterways crisscross Panama but only two rivers are navigable.

Nationalism and anti-U.S. sentiments have been a constant feature of Panamanian society since independence in 1903. In 1964, 21 Panamanians lost their lives to U.S. bullets to the gain right to fly the Panamanian flag at schools in the Canal Zone. But there is also, especially among the middle and upper classes, a pattern of dependent behavior and identification with all things with a USA label—from consumer products and cultural values to language and politics. It was no surprise to see many middle-class Panamanians out in the streets waving U.S. flags after the December 1989 invasion. It will also be no surprise to see the undercurrent of nationalism and resentment of the United States surge again in the near future.

Alienation distorts the Panamanian culture and society. Panamanians often feel like foreigners in their own country. The pervasive use of English in business and government and the use of the U.S. dollar as the national currency are constant reminders that their nation is not wholly their own. As Latin America expert John Weeks has written, "It is the curse of the collective consciousness of the Panamanian nation that it can take no pride in its formal creation, and that its founding fathers are justifiably branded as agents of a foreign power."[2]

Chapter 1

Politics

Government

The swearing in of President Guillermo Endara on a U.S. military base in Panama on December 20, 1989 marked the beginning of a new era of governance in Panama. For the first time since 1968 government in Panama was not beholden to the country's military. Endara and his two vice presidents — the candidates of the Democratic Civic Opposition Alliance (ADOC) — were the apparent winners of the May 7, 1989 election that was annulled by Gen. Manuel Antonio Noriega. The new civilian government, while breaking the two-decade tradition of military rule, renewed another more deeply rooted tradition in Panama: U.S. military intervention in the country's internal politics.

The Endara administration took office without real power and without an independent political platform. It was a government produced by a U.S. military invasion and one whose stability depended on a U.S. military occupation. The ADOC coalition had attracted more voters not because of the charisma or credibility of its candidates but rather as a result of the widespread unpopularity of Noriega and his puppets and the deep popular frustration with military governments.

Ushered into office by U.S. troops, the Endara government had little to offer the Panamanian people aside from a return to the politics of pre-Torrijos Panama with an agenda dictated by its U.S. benefactors and the country's business elite. Endara's first official communication was sent by a U.S. government fax machine, his cabinet members were chauffeured in U.S. embassy vehicles, and the new government was unable to occupy the presidential palace because it had been taken over by the U.S. military command.

The new government hoped to fill the void left by the collapse of the Noriega dictatorship. After two decades the system of government shaped by Omar Torrijos Herrera had exhausted its capability to maintain a ruling alliance. Although initially counting on the good will of Panamanians elated to see Noriega gone, the post-invasion government did not face an easy future. None of the parties in the ADOC coalition could count on a strong network of support among the urban and rural poor. Having come together as a broad alliance of business, civic, and political groups with the goal of ousting Noriega, the coalition had never ironed out a common political platform. Upon taking power, the personal and political differences among the three parties and their powerful supporters immediately began to weaken the coalition.

While ADOC celebrated an end to 21 years of military rule, it could not point to a pre-1968 period of stability and progress. From 1903 to 1968 Panama saw a series of elitist governments, none of which made a serious effort to assert Panamanian sovereignty or to institute serious social reforms.[1] Stability was based on collaboration with the U.S. military and repressive use of the country's own National Guard. It remains to be seen if the country's new rulers can overcome the elitist, and dependent behavior of the past to create a truly democratic system and thriving economy.

Legal Structure of Government

According to the 1983 constitution, executive power is held by a president directly elected every five years and assisted by two elected vice presidents and an appointed cabinet. Legislative power is vested in a unicameral Legislative Assembly. The government's judiciary branch comprises the Supreme Court, subordinate tribunals, and district and municipal courts.

Another important instrument of government is the Election Tribunal, an autonomous institution with representatives from the legislative, executive, and judicial branches and three elected judges. The country is divided into nine provinces, each with a governor appointed by the president, and it has one semi-autonomous Indian reservation. Each province is further divided into districts and municipalities.

For two decades Panama has had what is known as a decentralized government structure, comprising dozens of often highly corrupt state enterprises and sectoral institutions. These include a cement company, a racetrack, a sugar corporation, the telecommunications company, and a national lottery, as well as such institutions as the national university, the agricultural development bank, and the tourism bureau.

One of the most important of these state institutions is the Social Security Institute. Covering over half the population, Panama's social security system provides health service and financial benefits in cases of illness, accident, and maternity. It also pays funeral expenses and assists widows and orphans. Retiring workers receive monthly pensions ranging from $145 to $1000. During the 1980s structural-adjustment programs promoted by the World Bank, International Monetary Fund, and the U.S. Agency for International Development (AID) whittled away at the expansive public sector and further privatization is to be expected by the current U.S.-backed government.

Washington and the Government

The United States has played an important historic role in the governance of Panama. Since the mid-1850s, the United States has intervened militarily 18 times, sometimes to protect its own interests, other times to repress political dissent, and most recently to depose one government and install another. (See box on page 100.)

Although the Panamanian independence movement can be traced deep into the past century, it was Washington that made nationhood possible when it decided to build the canal there. But as Torrijos often remarked, the United States has too often behaved like a midwife who keeps the baby in return for her services.[2]

Even before Panamanian independence and the building of the canal, the United States had been in the habit of sending in troops to protect U.S. lives and interests. Between 1856 and 1903 the U.S. military intervened in Panama at least ten times. This custom of intervention became a right with the signing of the 1903 Hay-Bunau Varilla Treaty. This first canal treaty gave the United States the right to intervene militarily to "maintain public order necessary" for the construction and operation of the canal. It also gave the United States the power to act in the Canal Zone "as if it were the sovereign of the territory." A year later the country's new constitution established the United States as the guardian of Panamanian independence and sovereignty. The constitution gave Washington the right to intervene "in any part of Panama to reestablish public peace and constitutional order."[3]

From independence to 1936 Panama was treated as an unofficial protectorate of the United States. Adjustments were made in the dependency relationship that year when Presidents Franklin D. Roosevelt and Harmodio Arias Madrid signed a revised canal treaty that abrogated the U.S. right to intervene in the country's internal affairs.[4] The treaty also gave Panamanians increased access to the business of the Canal Zone — which previously had been exclusively in the hands of U.S. entrepreneurs.

Direct U.S. military intervention in Panama's internal affairs diminished after the 1936 treaty, and especially after the militarization of the Panamanian National Police in 1943. In 1964 U.S. troops were called in to control the riots that erupted after Balboa High School students and their parents (Zonians) tried to stop the raising of the Panamanian flag by Panamanian high school students. For the most part, though, the National Guard, created in 1953, has been able to maintain order without the need for U.S. troops.

When World War II came Panama was obliged to ally itself with the United States, and 130 U.S. military sites were established throughout Panama. Pressured by Panamanian business interests, another treaty revision was signed in 1955 which opened up increased commercial access to the Canal Zone. The canal and the surrounding zone, however, remained outside the Panamanian government's control.

Washington also exercised its influence in Panama through the oligarchy. The narrowly based oligarchy, whose members rotated in government until the mid-1930s, looked to the United States for its blessing of presidential candidates. In several cases, the oligarchy called for U.S. intervention to settle political disputes or to crush the popular movement. In 1944 a U.S. official noted that "there has never been a successful change of government in Panama but that American authorities have been consulted beforehand."[5]

After the 1977 signing of the new canal treaties, anti-U.S. sentiment abated. (See U.S. Foreign Policy) But during the 1980s the presence of the U.S. Southern Command (SOUTHCOM) in Panama and perceived violation of the treaties continued to fuel Panamanian nationalism. The economic structural-adjustment program imposed upon the Panamanian government by the World Bank and International Monetary Fund (IMF) and strongly supported by Washington gave rise to renewed nationalist sentiment.

Immediately after the 1984 presidential election Washington hailed the "successful transition" to democratic rule. Secretary of State George Shultz traveled to the inauguration of Nicolás Ardito Barletta to demonstrate U.S. support for the new president despite the patent fraudulence of the election. When political dissident and "freedom fighter" Hugo Spadafora was killed a year later, Washington remained conspicuously silent.[6]

For most of the decade U.S. attention was focused elsewhere in Central America, principally on Nicaragua. It feared that any U.S. challenge to Noriega might destabilize the internal political situation in Panama, obstruct the expanded use of U.S. military bases for operations in Nicaragua and El Salvador, and undermine collaborative military and intelligence operations with the country's military forces. But when

Noriega proved resistant to increased cooperation in the contra war, Washington suddenly reversed its Panama foreign policy and set out to topple the country's strongman. (See U.S. Foreign Policy) Harsh economic sanctions, military intimidation, support for the political opposition, and international isolation were Washington's new instruments of intervention.

Having failed to topple the Noriega regime through nonmilitary means, Washington launched a full-scale military invasion on December 20, 1989 involving more than 26,000 troops. The invasion succeeded in "decapitating" the Noriega government but it also leveled the infrastructure of government. For 21 years the Panamanian military had been the guiding institution in government. Not only had the Panamanian Defense Forces (PDF) served as the country's army but also as its police. The PDF (until 1983 called the National Guard) had succeeded during the 1970s in shaping a national coalition around the politics of nationalism and populism. It had brought important sectors of the national bourgeoisie into the coalition through its support and promotion of local industries and had opened the economy up to a new financial elite.

The U.S. invasion, justified as an effort to remove one strongman, pushed Panamanian political history back by more than half a century. Once again both the government and the security forces were heavily dependent and effectively controlled by Washington. The unifying principles of populism and nationalism, which had served for more than two decades to stabilize Panamanian politics and society, lay shattered. By so egregiously violating the 1977 treaties' prohibition of U.S. intervention in the country's internal political affairs, an old wound was reopened. Not only did the future control of the canal once again become an unresolved issue but the country's very sovereignty also became an open question.

Oligarchy and the Government

Before 1968 politics in Panama were dominated by the country's small oligarchy—a grouping of a couple dozen families that are known disparagingly as *rabiblancos* or white tails.[7] For the most part this elite represented the service and commercial sector associated with the transit operations of the canal. Less powerful were the large landowners and cattle ranchers. (See Economy)

Political parties in Panama have served as clubs of the oligarchy.[8] The two main political clubs of the 1800s were the Liberal and Conservative Parties of Colombia. Even after independence these two elite political groups continued to compete for office. Having no serious political differences with the Liberals, Panamanian Conservatives disbanded in 1912 and integrated themselves into one or another Liberal Party faction.

When elections approached, various offshoots of the Liberal Party formed to support individual candidates. More than a half-dozen different versions of the Liberal Party governed between 1903 and 1968. There was little real difference between any of the competing factions. Parties were based on personalities and promised favors rather than contrasting political platforms.[9]

Arnulfo Arias:

Next to Omar Torrijos, Arnulfo Arias Madrid was Panama's most imposing politician. It was Arias (1901-1988) who first seized upon nationalism and populism as a winning political formula in Panama. Beginning in the 1930s Arnulfo and his brother Harmodio Arias presented a nagging challenge to the country's political establishment. While disputing the political stronghold of the Liberal Party, the Arias brothers never challenged the economic privileges of the oligarchy.

Arnulfo Arias, soon eclipsing his older brother, took politics out of the clubhouse. With his populist and nationalistic rhetoric, Arias established a popular base for politics in Panama. He tapped the long-breeding Panamanian resentment over U.S. control, while also calling for basic social reforms. Arnulfo Arias founded the *panameñista* movement which gathered popular support among small landholders and others resentful of the oligarchy's exclusionary politics. Although he espoused a populist program, Arias was more closely committed to the interests of the oligarchy than he was to the popular sectors. In particular he represented the more backward elements of Panamanian capitalism, for example: the landed elite, small entrepreneurs, and real estate interests.

He operated in many ways like a traditional *patrón*. Arias occasionally acted and spoke on behalf of the interests of the popular sectors and helped modernize Panamanian government. But never did he stand behind the kind of structural reforms needed to alter the country's narrow class structure or to integrate the popular sectors into the political process as full participants. Arias served as president three times and was deposed each time by changing alliances of the traditional political elite, the National Guard, and the U.S. embassy. The charismatic figure was also denied the presidency in two fraudulent elections — the latest one being in 1984.[11]

The oligarchy ruled at the pleasure of the U.S. authorities and relied on the might of the U.S. military to maintain the peace. "The overwhelming dominance of American governments over Panama distorted political life both between the rulers and the ruled and within the elite itself," observed John Weeks. "Relieved of the burden of consolidating its rule over the population, the Panamanian elite failed to develop effective, long-term institutions of political accommodation and cooptation."[10]

A Wild Card in Panamanian Politics

Until his death Arias remained the country's most popular politician. For many years he successfully tapped the paranoia and deep resentment that Panamanians harbored as a result of having their country occupied and often directly controlled by foreigners. During his brief stint as president in 1941, Arias decreed that all advertising be in Spanish. In his xenophobic zeal, Arias also appealed to widespread racism among Panamanians against Caribbean blacks and other immigrants.

Like Arias, Torrijos also propagated the politics of populism and nationalism. But unlike Arias, Torrijos actually made a break from the oligarchy—something that Arias, a wealthy coffee grower himself, never tried to do. In the 1980s Arias, ever the political opportunist, dropped his anti-U.S. rhetoric. Instead he focused his vitriol on the Panamanian military and succeeded in capturing the country's swelling antimilitarist sentiment. He disdained the Civic Crusade's dependency on Washington and was running as an independent presidential candidate on the ticket of his own Authentic Panameñista Party (PPA) when he died in 1988.

For almost a half century Arias injected a kind of messianic appeal into political campaigning in Panama.[12] Before 1968 this zeal was directed against the country's traditional political parties and later against those associated with the military. In the end, however, *panameñismo* was based more on personality than on a political platform. His charisma and populist rhetoric obscured the PPA's elitist character and lack of a popular based party infrastructure. After Arias died, the PPA split into two factions (with the encouragement and manipulation of the Noriega government) with one side staying in the 1989 election as an independent party and the other faction, led by Guillermo Endara, joining the U.S.-backed political ADOC coalition.

When the National Guard took control over the government in 1968, the oligarchy lacked a unifying vision of economic progress and modernization. Although breaking the dominance of the oligarchy, the Torrijos regime did not represent a class-based attack on the private sector. Instead it set about establishing a new economic alliance with the industrial and financial sectors, bypassing the interests of some of the more traditional oligarchic sectors. Many representatives of the private sector were brought into the Torrijos government as cabinet ministers and Torrijos worked closely with business leaders in developing the international financial center, expanding the Colón Free Zone, and developing the country's industrial and agricultural production capacity.

Since 1964 the National Council of Private Enterprise (CONEP) has served as the private sector's principal lobbying organization. CONEP was formed by the Chamber of Commerce, the Panamanian Association of Panamanian Business Executives (APEDE), and other business organizations to function as a type of ministry without portfolio to be consulted by the government prior to the enactment of laws that would affect the private sector.[13] Until 1968 CONEP functioned as planned but during the early years of the Torrijos regime CONEP lost its privileged place in economic policymaking. After 1968 the association focused on defeating or reversing Torrijos populist initiatives. CONEP, for example, played a key role in revising the Labor Code in 1976 and in blocking the proposed educational reform in 1979.

Torrijos succeeded in establishing a close alliance with the industrial bourgeoisie and those financial interests associated with the country's international services economy. After his death, representatives of the traditional parties were brought back into the government's political alliance for the 1984 elections. Joining the National Democratic Union (UNADE) were the Liberal and Republican parties, the business-oriented and military-created Panamanian Labor Party (PALA), and the Revolutionary Democratic Party (PRD). The choice of Ardito Barletta, while opposed by the *torrijista* factions of the PRD, was the choice of Noriega and widely supported by the business community. The replacement of Ardito Barletta, who was pushed out of office in 1985, by misfit Vice President Erick Arturo Delvalle, a multimillionaire with interests in sugar, race horses, and television, also illustrated the close working relationship that existed between the government and oligarchy.

Beginning in mid-1987 the country's dominant economic forces began grouping around the National Civic Crusade and later the Democratic Opposition Alliance (ADOC). The Civic Crusade brought together dozens of civic groups, business organizations, and professional associations. Three opposition political parties also were closely associated with the Civic Crusade: Christian Democratic Party (PDC), Authentic Panameñista Party (PPA), and the Popular Action Party (PAPO). By 1988 it was also becoming clear that the country's powerful financial sector, which for so long had supported the military government, had moved into the opposition. It was not, however, the oligarchs who were the main activists of the Civic Crusade. Its most active supporters were found among the country's merchant class, landowners, middle classes, and small business entrepreneurs.

Elements of the oligarchy closely involved in the military business complex, like the Duque family, favored continuing the alliance with the National Guard. Although not supporters of Noriega, the financial sector did not immediately throw its support behind the U.S.-guided Civic Crusade. Washington's attempts since the early 1980s to break down the country's bank secrecy laws were strongly rejected by the banking community and widely regarded as being part of a U.S. campaign to undermine Panamanian sovereignty. The Civic Crusade's initial backing of U.S. economic sanctions angered large sectors of the Panamanian elite and obstructed the construction of a unified upper-class alliance against Noriega.

There was, however, wide agreement among the oligarchy and those supporting the Civic Crusade that Noriega must go and the Panamanian Defense Forces be returned to their barracks. Instead of playing a direct role in government, all sectors of the oligarchy—except those directly linked with the PDF in business transactions—wanted the military to step down from its central role in government and resume its pre-1968 role as the armed guarantor of political stability and elite rule. With the installation of the Endara government, the country's economic elite again assumed direct control over the country's economic and political development.

Military and the Government

The U.S. military invasion of 1989 brought to an end a 21-year period in which the military exercised direct or indirect control over government in Panama. More than armed might backed up those decades of military rule. The principles and practices of *torrijismo* allowed the military to govern without resorting to the widespread repression and human rights violations common to most military-run governments. By the late 1980s, however, *torrijismo* was little more than the empty rhetoric used to justify continued corrupt rule by the PDF and its puppet politicians. The dissolution of the PDF in December 1989 left a gaping hole in Panamanian government. This recalled the first years of Panamanian nationhood when the country's military was dissolved by the United States which itself assumed the responsibility for maintaining internal order and defending the newly independent country.

For three decades after independence the Panamanian police were kept at this lowly and largely subservient status. The police, mainly from *mestizo* rural origins, were labeled as *cholos*.[14] As a result of a revised canal treaty in 1936, Washington relinquished its right to intervene militarily in the country's internal affairs. President Harmodio Arias appointed José Antonio Remón Cantera to be chief of police in 1943, and under Remón's reign the prestige and the power of the National Police Forces steadily increased.

By the mid-1940s the national police was a power in its own right and had become the chief arbiter of power in the political arena.[15] Under Remón the police brokered disputes among the oligarchy and colluded with certain factions. In 1952 Remón stepped down as police chief and ran successfully for president as the head of a new conservative political coalition called the National Patriotic Committee (CPN). The police (called the National Guard after 1953) did not participate directly in government but increasingly served in its repressive capacity as the guarantor of oligarchic rule. A faction of the Liberal Party joined with the CPN to sweep the 1956 election, and two National Liberal party candidates—Roberto Chiari (1960-1964) and Marco Robles (1964-1968)—held presidential office in the 1960s.

Although the economy was expanding, Panama in the late 1960s was facing a hegemonic crisis.[16] The traditional political parties were badly divided and counted on little support among the popular sectors which had become increasingly restive. The election of maverick politician Arnulfo Arias in 1968 was unhappily received by the National Guard and the traditional Liberal parties. The National Guard saw Arias as a threat to the power and privileges it had been accumulating through close relations with the oligarchy. Having heard that Arias planned to restructure the guard and remove many of its officers, the National Guard ousted the president.

In the jousting for dominance following 1968, Omar Torrijos Herrera emerged as the dominant figure. Torrijos, a son of middle-class educators in rural Panama, became the National Guard's third commander-in-chief and the first not linked familially to the oligarchy.[17] Under the provisions of the 1972 constitution, Torrijos became head of government. In 1978 Aristides Royo was elected by the National Assembly to become the country's figurehead president. Until his death in a mysterious airplane crash in July 1981, Torrijos was the center of political and military power in Panama. With many of the characteristics of a traditional *caudillo*, Torrijos ruled Panama with a strong but considerate hand. Years after his death many Panamanians still had photos of Torrijos hanging in a place of honor on their living room walls.

Raising high the banners of nationalism and populism, Torrijos proceeded to restructure Panamanian government and politics. The traditional political parties and the Legislative Assembly were abolished. The National Guard, at least until the mid-1970s, became an autonomous political force that ruled the country with the consultation and assistance of leaders of the private and popular sectors. Progressives and communists were brought into government mainly in the ministries of education, labor, health, agricultural development, and foreign policy while representatives of the business sector were appointed to positions in planning, finance, and commerce and industry.[18]

For the first time, government institutions were opened up to participation by *mestizos*, blacks, and those with lower-class origins. Calling himself *"cholo* Omar," Torrijos won wide popular support from formerly disenfranchised sectors of the population.

Another characteristic of the Torrijos regime and subsequent governments in Panama is what some have called the "military-business complex."[19] Although he broke the stronghold of the oligarchy on government, Torrijos encouraged the participation and cooperation of the industrial and financial sectors of the economic elite in his government. In return the National Guard leadership corps enriched themselves with favors and bribes offered by the private sector. The extensive network of state enterprises that was developed during the Torrijos regime also offered a new source of wealth for ambitious officers. The Transit Corporation and Colón Free Zone were especially lucrative targets for National Guard corruption. Because of their involvement in gambling, prostitution, and vice businesses, National Guard officers have been called the "mafia chiefs" of Panama.[20]

The 1972 constitution inscribed the new-found power of the National Guard into the law of the land. Previously the National Guard was subject to the constitutional civilian government, but the new Magna Carta stipulated that "the three governmental branches are obligated to act in harmonious collaboration with the public force [National Guard]." Among the important new government institutions were the National Assembly of Community Representatives, the National Legislative Council, Legislating Commission, and local community boards under the direction of the General Directorate for Community Development (DIGEDE-

COM). The new institutions, especially the community boards and the National Assembly, permitted popular sectors to participate in government for the first time. But legislative and executive power was concentrated in the hands of General Torrijos.

For many Panamanian political analysts the Torrijos regime never fully committed itself to the popular sectors. Rather it was, as Marco Gandásegui describes it, a government of pacification which by coopting the popular sectors permitted the most advanced sectors of the bourgeoisie to execute projects of capital accumulation without concern for social upheaval and political unrest.[21] Leftist critics of the regime also charged that even the nationalism of *torrijismo* has been much overrated. The 1977 Canal Treaties, for example, continued to compromise the country's sovereignty and Torrijos' promotion of Panama as a platform of transnational services further increased the country's state of economic dependency.

Although the National Guard was in fact the country's main political institution, few guardsmen actually held government posts. One exception to this rule was Rubén Darío Paredes who served as Minister of Agricultural Development in 1975.[22] Torrijos' fellow officers were not brought into the government apparatus but more than 30 friends and family members were given key positions within his government — one reason explaining the extraordinary stability of the regime.[23] Another element in the Torrijos regime and subsequent military-controlled governments was the participation of such dedicated technocrats as Ardito Barletta who became Planning Minister and in 1984 rose to the presidency.

Responding to local and international pressure, Torrijos in 1978 took steps to return Panama to civilian rule. An official party, the Democratic Revolutionary Party (PRD), was created to compete in local elections scheduled for 1980 and the presidential election set for 1984. The PRD was conceived as a centrist political party that would administer the Panamanian state with the politics of pragmatism and cooptation much like the corporatist Institutional Revolutionary Party (PRI) of Mexico.

The PRD, however, quickly proved incapable of this challenge. In the 1980 elections for the Legislative Council the party faced a strong antimilitarist challenge from the Christian Democratic Party and reconstituted Liberal factions. Arnulfo Arias and his *panameñista* movement also challenged the legitimacy of the National Guard-PRD controlled state.[24] While the popular sectors did not break with the government, the gap between the regime's populist rhetoric and its private-sector oriented policies was widening.

The populism and nationalism of *torrijismo* effectively disappeared from government with the death of Torrijos. After 1981 the Panamanian government became steadily more conservative. In contrast to the 1970s when the National Guard prided itself for its role in establishing a more independent foreign policy, the guard leadership between 1981 and 1987 allowed U.S. military forces to use Panama as a base for an intervention in Central America.

Three National Guard officers—Noriega, Paredes, and Díaz Herrera—became contenders for political and military leadership after Torrijos' death. Apparently the three agreed to alternate in power. As National Guard commander, Paredes challenged the independence of the PRD and in July 1982 removed Torrijos' hand-picked president, Aristides Royo, and replaced him with Ricardo De La Espriella. Paredes meanwhile also began to extend his power base by trying to bring disaffected elements of the private sector, mainly the agricultural oligarchy, into a new political alliance. But when Paredes retired from the guard to run for president, Noriega did not support his bid—which left Paredes marginalized and extremely bitter. As the new National Guard commander, Noriega engineered to have Ardito Barletta run for president as part of a five-party coalition.

The fraudulent nature of democracy in Panama became obvious to all who wanted to see in September 1984 when Nicolás Ardito Barletta was inaugurated president after the country's first national election in 16 years. Once again Arnulfo Arias was denied the presidency despite an apparent electoral victory. In the face of rising public protest to his austerity program, Ardito Barletta was deposed a year later by Noriega and replaced with Erick Arturo Delvalle. For three years years Delvalle proved a faithful servant of Noriega.

In February 1988, however, Delvalle tried to replace Noriega as PDF commander. Instead it was Delvalle who was forced to step down. In his place, Noriega appointed Manuel Solís Palma to the presidency. Solís Palma finished out the five-year term started by Ardito Barletta. In September 1989 Noriega appointed Francisco Rodríguez to be provisional president; and then in December 1989 Noriega was declared head of government by the newly appointed National Assembly.[25]

Omar Torrijos launched a government of "new politics" in Panama distinguished by the military's central role in not only maintaining the stability of the state but also setting its domestic and foreign policies. By establishing the PRD, Torrijos hoped to create a political infrastructure to continue the policies of *torrijismo*. These can be summarized as follows: a nonaligned foreign policy with a strong nationalist flavor, populist reforms that give formerly disenfranchised sectors access to government and allow them to more fully participate in economic growth, expanded state intervention in the economy, and an alliance with the modernizing sector of the private elite (mainly industry and the international service sectors).

Only the shell of the new politics was left by early 1980s. The military's earlier success in stabilizing the state, giving the economy new direction, and incorporating the popular sectors had given way to a new crisis of state. Symptomatic of this crisis was the quick turnover of Panamanian presidents from 1982 to 1989: Royo, De La Espriella, Ardito Barletta, Delvalle, Solís Palma, and Rodríguez. At each step the civilian government became more a puppet of the military. Finally the facade of a civilian government was thrown aside in December 1989 when the resurrected National Assembly of Community Representatives, largely composed of PRD functionaries, declared Noriega head of government.

Government had come full circle by the end of the decade. Once again the commander of the military was also the country's top figure in government. To legitimize this new military government, Noriega, like Torrijos before him, identified himself with the politics of nationalism and populism. Noriega's credentials as a populist and nationalist leader were, however, even less convincing. His recent history, joint military maneuvers with U.S. forces, the increasing repression of workers, and his support for antipopular austerity measures all undermined Noriega's ability to portray himself as a leader in the *torrijista* tradition.

Popular Sectors and the Government

Before 1968 the working classes and the popular movements of unions, peasant organizations, students, leftist parties, and community organizations had been effectively excluded from the political system. When the popular movements seemed to be gathering too much strength, they were repressed either by local or U.S. security forces. The oligarchic parties paid little attention to the demands of the popular sectors, preferring instead to administer politics and the economy in the traditional exclusionary fashion.

A constant threat to the inertia of the oligarchy was the *panameñista* movement of Arnulfo Arias, a populist leader who received support among the lower classes for his support of social reforms. (See Political Parties) Although Arias did push through significant reforms during his brief moments in power, he made no effort to incorporate the popular sectors into the political system. In contrast, Torrijos, also a populist, adopted a series of measures that for the first time brought workers and peasants into the circles of political power.

Once having secured his dominant place within the National Guard, Torrijos established an alliance with the communist People's Party. As the country's the most militant defender of worker and peasant rights, the People's Party was the organization most capable of mobilizing popular support for the new regime. In exchange for the party's collaboration, Torrijos brought worker and peasant activists into the new political structures established by his regime.

In the countryside, Torrijos revived the country's agrarian reform by promoting settlements (*asentamientos campesinos*) of landless peasants on lands secured by the government. The People's Party, whose student branch had already been been drawn into an alliance with the government, was given a leading role in the National Confederation of Peasant Settlements (CONAC).[26] Besides representing the interests of the peasant settlements, CONAC, established in 1970s, also served as a consultative body about peasant affairs and a focus for pro-Torrijos mobilizing.

Torrijos singled out the labor sector for his most concerted efforts to build popular support for his government.[27] The pro-union Labor Code of 1972 and the formation of National Council of Workers (CONATO) were the main initiatives to incorporate unions into the new government alliance sponsored by the National Guard. Previously repressed and isolated, the labor movement was given official recognition and support. The newly established Ministry of Labor was obligated by the new Labor Code "to promote the establishment of unions in the areas or sectors where they are lacking." Union leaders, particularly those from the leftist and more militant National Council of Panamanian Workers (CNTP), were consulted about labor and other government policies and appointed to government positions.

The Torrijos regime also attempted to defuse potential unrest among the marginal communities by incorporating them into government structures. A good example of this policy was the regime's initiatives in the explosive shantytown of San Miguelito. Located northeast of Panama City, San Miguelito was the focus of much progressive community organizing by Catholic priests. The government made San Miguelito a special autonomous municipality separate from Panama City. This opened the way for greater political and economic participation on the part of the squatters of San Miguelito.[28]

Popular access to political power was institutionalized through a new system of political representation authorized by the 1972 constitution.

Torrijos disbanded the Legislative Assembly and abolished the traditional political parties. In their place, he established the National Assembly
of Community Representatives on the national level and a network of
community boards on the local level, with one board for each one of the
505 *corregimientos* or local political districts. At each level of the hierarchy, popular representatives were to have a role in government along with
appointed government officials.[29]

By the mid-1970s, however, the strong commitment to popular political participation demonstrated by Torrijos during his first years in power
had substantially faded. The regime had successfully coopted most of the
popular sectors by giving them unprecedented political access and
government recognition. But the economic downturn, increased private-
sector pressure, and bureaucratic resistance combined to undermine the
kind of inclusionary initiatives demonstrated by the government, especially from 1970 to 1974.

CONAC was defunded and land distribution to the *asentamientos* was
sharply reduced. The government turned against labor, acceding to pressure from the private sector to revise the Labor Code in 1976, and CON-
ATO was kept powerless by ideological and turf battles. The National
Assembly of Community Representatives was more of a sounding board
than a legislative branch of government.[30] It was consistently denied
decision-making power and often treated patronizingly by the government ministries. The community boards frequently found themselves
powerless in the face of the appointed *corregidores* and local economic
elites. They were also frustrated in their economic initiatives by lack of
cooperation and assistance by government ministries on which they
depended for funding and technical help.

Although the reformism of *torrijismo* had lost momentum by the mid-
1970s and was moribund by 1981, the military-controlled governments of
the 1980s were able to dip into this historic political alliance with the
popular sectors. Collaboration with the Torrijos regime had coopted and
pacified most popular leaders and popular organizations. When faced
with the U.S. destablization campaign, Noriega was able to tap these
coopted sectors to support the ruling coalition. CONATO, for example,
supported the government's COLINA coalition in the 1989 presidential
election in return for government appointments and a greater share of
representation in the National Assembly. But at the national university,
banners and graffiti proclaiming "Neither *rabiblancos* nor the dictatorship" expressed a popular rejection of both the government and the U.S.-
backed opposition.

Political Parties and Elections

Since 1968 the military had functioned as de facto political party and its leaders as political leaders.[31] By installing the new government of Guillermo Endara in 1989, the United States assumed its historic role as a leading protagonist in the internal politics of Panama. After more than two decades of military rule, the government was headed by politicians independent of Panamanian military.

The Endara-headed ADOC coalition had won the May 1989 presidential election by a two-to-one margin according to most foreign and domestic election monitors but was denied victory by General Noriega. Amidst ensuing international condemnation of the fraudulent and violent nature of the election, the regime canceled the results of the election. The United States insisted that Erick Delvalle, ousted in February 1988, was still the legitimate president of Panama. In September 1989, when the former presidential term expired, Noriega selected Francisco Rodríguez as provisional president, while Washington declared that Endara should have been inaugurated as the country's new president.

The new administration installed after the U.S. invasion in December 1989 was that of the Democratic Opposition Alliance, an opposition alliance of three political parties and various civic organizations. President Guillermo Endara was a founding member of the Authentic Panameñista Party (PPA), a conservative populist party headed by Arnulfo Arias until his death in 1988. First vice president is Ricardo Arias Calderón, president of the Christian Democratic Party (PDC). Second vice president is Guillermo Ford of the National Liberal Republican Movement (MOLIRENA), a fusion of the traditional Liberal Party factions of the oligarchy.

Although the ADOC political coalition clearly received more votes than the government coalition in the May 1989 elections, none of the three parties represented in the coalition could point to a strong popular base and party infrastructure. "The vote is not for individual candidates," explained Alfredo Maduro, president of the Chamber of Commerce, "It is for Noriega or change."[32]

Traditionally in Panamanian politics, there has been no strong party infrastructure that remains in place between elections. Parties and political coalitions often disintegrate after elections and emerge again with new names with the opening of a new political campaign. A further weakness of Panamanian politics is the lack of detailed political platforms. In 1968 the National Guard brushed aside the country's political parties and substituted its own authority and populist ideology. With the military gone as

the society's strongest institution, the responsibility of governing once
again fell upon the country's weak political parties.

Pre-December 1989 Pro-Government Parties

Seven political parties joined the pro-government National Liberation
Coalition (COLINA) to contest the May 1989 elections. They were:
Democratic Revolutionary Party (PRD), Republican Party, Liberal
Party, Panama Labor Party (PALA), People's Party, Democratic
Workers Party, and the Revolutionary Panama Party. The PRD was
founded in 1978 by General Torrijos in hopes of forming a statist party
that would direct Panama much as the PRI in Mexico has done. The
military also joined with certain business interests to create PALA in 1982
to promote the candidacy of General Paredes.

COLINA represented a regrouping of the National Democratic
Union (UNADE) coalition that ran Ardito Barletta as the pro-government candidate in 1984. Ardito Barletta and his two vice presidents, Erick
Delvalle and Roderick Esquivel, represented the conservative and pro-
business wing of the government coalition. As the 1989 elections approached and the U.S. destabilization campaign intensified, government
and the UNADE parties tried to distance themselves from the antipopular policies adopted by the Ardito Barletta and Delvalle administra-
tions. The more conservative elements of the UNADE coalition were not
included in COLINA. PRD spokesperson Nils Castro said that post-
election government would return to "authentic *torrijismo*" and would be
"more class-oriented, more anti-oligarchy, and more anti-imperialist."
The coalition tried to appeal to Panamanian nationalism with the slogan:
"COLINA not Colonia."

Carlos Duque, who had close business relationships with the PDF,
was COLINA's presidential candidate. He was president of the military-
run television station and directed the Transit Company, a giant scam that
attached revenue stamps to import-export documents. COLINA's election bid was backed by such popular-sector organizations as CONATO,
CONAC, Coordinator of Public Sector Unions, and a large public-sector
federation called FENASEP.

The Democratic Opposition Civic Alliance

The Democratic Opposition Civic Alliance (ADOC) represented a
merger of the Democratic Opposition Alliance (ADO) and the Civic
Crusade. ADO was the antigovernment political coalition that ran Arnulfo Arias as its presidential candidate in 1984. Besides Arias' PPA, ADO
included the Christian Democratic Party (PDC) and the National Liberal

Republican Movement (MOLIRENA). The Civic Crusade was formed in June 1987 by a group of anti-government business owners to capitalize on the spontaneous popular demonstrations that resulted from charges by Col. Roberto Díaz Herrera linking Noriega to the torture and murder of former Vice Minister of Health Hugo Spadafora, and the fraudulent character of the 1984 elections.[33]

In 1984 the candidacy of the ever-popular Arnulfo Arias accounted for the strong showing of the ADO coalition. Widening dissatisfaction with the ruling government coalition after 1984 created a yet wider voter base for the opposition coalition in the 1989 election. Besides the Civic Crusade, ADOC included MOLIRENA, the PDC, and the backers of the deceased Arnulfo Arias. The ADOC coalition was also supported by dissidents from the Liberal Parties (Roderick Esquivel) and the Republican Party (Erick Delvalle). In addition, ADOC counted on the strong support of the Catholic church. The ADOC coalition apparently won the election by a wide margin based on a broad public rejection of Manuel Noriega.

The ADOC slate (Endara, Calderón, and Ford), installed as the new government of Panama in late 1989, has promised to rule by consensus. But in this New Right political coalition Calderón will likely emerge as the strongest figure.

ADOC's presidential candidate Guillermo Endara Galimany, born in 1936, studied law at New York University and before becoming a leader of the opposition was professor of business law at the University of Panama and a partner in a major law firm of which he was a founding member. Endara never held a post in government before becoming president. In 1964 he helped found the Panameñista Party and served as a close adviser to Arnulfo Arias until Arias' death in 1988. When Arias died the opposition looked to his widow to run as presidential candidate but when she proved to have no political experience or interest the opposition turned to Endara. During the election campaign Endara made no secret that he frequently consulted with the U.S. embassy—as many as three times daily—and he was ushered into the presidency by U.S. troops.

The *amulfista* faction that Endara represents is the weakest in the ADOC coalition. Besides holding the presidency, this faction heads a small number of state institutions and has little presence in the Legislative Assembly. Endara and the *amulfistas* do not control the levers of political power.

The **Christian Democratic Party (PDC)** is one of the most conservative Christian Democratic parties in the region. Led by Ricardo Arias Calderón, the PDC has closely associated itself with U.S. policy and strategy in Panama. Arias Calderón, a philosophy teacher turned politician, is known as the "holy nun" within the country because of his sanctimonious behavior and lack of charisma. Arias Calderón, 57, is a Yale University graduate and was a professor at Florida International University in Miami. The PDC's base is found among the middle class, professionals, and the financial community. The party's former commitment to the interests of the poor majority and to forging a new and more broadly based politics of national development have been dropped in favor of a private-sector oriented approach to economic development and a political direction that is closely associated with the U.S. State Department.

In the post-invasion government the PDC is the most well-prepared and powerful party. Not only does it have the most consistent and appealing political rhetoric and the most international support, it also counts on the majority of the national legislators and the ministries of Government and Justice, Education, and Housing and Public Works. The PDC also controls such state institutions as INTEL, IRHE, INDE, IMA, National Cultural Institute, and the Immigration agency.

The **National Liberal Republican Movement (MOLIRENA)** formed the third pillar of the ADOC alliance. Represented by Guillermo Ford, MOLIRENA formed in 1984 as a coalition of traditional oligarchic political parties not associated with the government. A rightwing party, MOLIRENA brought together the factions of the Liberal, National, and Republican Parties that stood outside the government's own political coalition. Ford and MOLIRENA will be the driving force behind the neoliberal economic policy of the Endara government – a policy synthesized by Vice President Ford: "Panama will be a country that is 100 percent private property."[34] In the new government, MOLIRENA controls the ministries of Planning and Economy, Treasury, Labor, and Social Welfare. It also runs the government's General Accounting department, the National Lottery, and the ministries of Health and Foreign Relations.

Independent Parties

Besides ADOC and COLINA, the **Authentic Panameñista Party (PPA)** also contended for power in the May 1989 elections. Following the death of party patriarch Arnulfo Arias in August 1988, the PPA split into two factions. The Endara faction left the party to form the Authentic Liberal Party (PLA) and join the U.S.-backed opposition. The remnants of the party regrouped under the leadership of party Secretary General Hildebrando Nicosia Pérez. The reconstructed party recognized the legitimacy of the Solís Palma government and was strongly critical of U.S. economic sanctions. It posed as the rightful heir of the legacy of nationalism and populism left by Arias.

Left-of-Center Parties

Panama's communist and socialist parties were at the heart of most popular antigovernment and labor organizing from the 1920s to the late 1960s. But during the period of military rule (1969-1989) the organized left in Panama became closely associated with the government.

People's Party (PP): Founded in 1930 as an outgrowth of the Communist Group of the the Panamanian Workers Federation, the PP is the country's Moscow-linked communist party. There had been widespread communist sympathies among Panamanian workers since the Russian Revolution of 1917 but the difference between the anarcho-syndicalists and the Bolshevik sympathizers kept the left divided and incapable of forming a party. Originally called the Communist Party, it changed its name in 1943 and was successful in organizing broad popular and labor protests in the 1940s. At the same time the party became a powerful presence among the banana workers of United Fruit. Also during the 1940s the PP was instrumental in establishing the FSTRP labor federation which was later became the CNTP. Following the Cuban Revolution in 1959 two militant factions broke off from the PP to form the National Vanguard Action (VAN) and the Revolutionary University Movement (MUR).

Throughout its history the PP had been subject to government repression. At the outset of the 1968 coup, the new military regime hunted out and arrested PP leaders, seeing them as its potential enemies. The PP's two offshoots — MUR and VAN — formed the National Liberation Movement (MLN) to resist the new military government. The rural insurgency was quickly eliminated but the urban MLN units kept up the fight for almost a year. Leftist resistance to the military regime disintegrated, however, when Torrijos began bringing the PP into its nationalist and populist alliance. Numerous PP members were given government positions by Torrijos. In return, the PP mobilized popular support for the military government. In 1984 the PP broke away from the pro-government UNADE alliance and ran its own candidate because of the government's sharp departure from the principles of *torrijismo*. By the 1989 elections, however, the PP was back in the government fold.

Socialist Workers Party (PST): Like the PP, the Trotskyite PST was founded in 1930 by a branch of the Communist Group. The PST first took a stance parallel to that of the Civic Crusade but then worked with the antimilitary and anti-imperialist Popular Civic Movement (MCP), which was headed by Mauro Zuñiga who had organized anti-IMF protests in 1984-1985.[35] The PST's principal person in José Cambra.

Revolutionary Workers Party (PRT): The PRT, another small socialist party, had offered critical support for the Noriega government. Its 1988 platform proposed the development of "a strong nationalism in the process of building a popular democracy." It was the PRT's position that the military had vacillated in its historic role of leading the popular alliance and creating a popular democracy.[36] Its leader is Graciela Dixon.

The Panamanian left is small, divided, and isolated. For the most part, it allowed itself and its associated popular organizations and unions to be coopted by the government. Its failure to develop an independent and class-based political platform is in part responsible for the country's lack of a progressive alternative to the oligarchy and the military. By adhering to a narrow nationalism promoted by the PDF and by not raising strong demands for democratic changes, it allowed the oligarchy, the church, and the New Right to lead the opposition to the military dictatorship.

Peace Process

Panama was one of the four founding nations of the Contadora peace initiative. Meeting on the island of Contadora off the coast of Panama in January 1983, Panama, along with Mexico, Venezuela, and Colombia, began the peace process which would eventually lead to the Esquipulas peace accords. Panama, anxious about the Reagan administration's apparent opposition to the Carter-Torrijos Canal Treaties, took an active role in the Contadora process, believing that this type of multilateral action would help guarantee the orderly transfer of the canal into Panamanian hands.

The Contadora peace process represented the growing Latin American independence from the dictates of U.S. foreign policy. In 1985 four additional Latin American nations (Brazil, Argentina, Uruguay, and Peru) joined the process. At a meeting of the eight nations in November 1987, Mexican Foreign Minister Bernardo Sepulveda Amor said: "This is the first opportunity in the entire history of the region in which eight Latin American heads of state are meeting through their own convocation and having determined the agenda themselves. In that sense, it is a political event of the utmost significance."[37]

Among the Contadora peace proposals were the withdrawal of military advisers, a ban on arms imports, restriction of foreign military exercises, the closure of foreign military bases, free elections, the establishment of verification commissions, and an end to foreign support of guerrilla movements.

In September 1984 Nicaragua accepted the first Contadora draft, catching the Untied States and the other Central American nations by surprise. Secretary of State George Shultz had called the proposed Contadora agreement "an important step forward" with many "positive elements" until Nicaragua accepted. At that point, Washington successfully worked to scuttle the Contadora process. Shultz called the agreement signed by Nicaragua "one-sided" and "unsatisfactory." In October 1984 the National Security Council was boasting, "We have effectively blocked Contadora group efforts....We have trumped the latest Nicaragua/ Mexican efforts to rush signature of an unsatisfactory Contadora agreement."[38]

The other Central American countries had given conditional acceptance to the agreement until Nicaragua actually signed it. Then, after Washington subjected them to intensive consultation, they too found imperfections in the agreement and refused to sign. The Contadora process continued for three more years, during which the U.S. government refused to make any binding commitment to the process and in fact repeatedly attempted to sabotage it.

Washington encouraged its four Central American allies to initiate their own peace process, over which it assumed it would have more control. But this regional peace process, which built on the Contadora experience, backfired and once again left the U.S. government fighting the peace initiative. Panama did not participate in the Esquipulas or subsequent regional peace negotiations. After the annulment of the May 1989 elections, the Organization of American States (OAS) tried unsuccessfully to mediate in negotiations between the government and the political opposition.

Human Rights

Human rights violations by the security forces and associated paramilitary groups have been widespread since 1987, although serious abuses, like torture, killings, and disappearances, were rare. Violent suppression of demonstrations, arbitrary short-term detentions, sexual abuses of detainees, and sharp limitations of freedom of press and expression constitute the most common violations.

It was not until the kidnapping and decapitation of Dr. Hugo Spadafora in 1985 that the human rights situation in Panama became a matter of great national and international concern. In 1987 the Inter-American Commission on Human Rights of the OAS accused certain members of the PDF of the crime, and in 1989 called for "an exhaustive investigation" into the assassination of Spadafora. The Panamanian government has repeatedly responded that, because the crime happened in Costa Rica, it has no jurisdiction.

The mutilation and death of Spadafora sparked internal criticism within the National Guard and popular protests. From June through August 1987, after the revelations of Colonel Díaz Herrera, there were large demonstrations marking the anniversary of Spadafora's death and the fraudulent elections, in which protesters also complained about other human rights violations by the PDF. The protests were brutally crushed by the "Dobermans," the PDF's anti-riot squads. Human rights violations increased steadily after the June 1987 events. Harassment of journalists and government control over the media became common.

Amnesty International charged the country's security forces with "excessive use of force" in response to anti-government demonstrations.[39] This includes the common practice of beating arrested demonstrators and critics of the government. Demonstrators also are subject to liberal use of birdshot by anti-riot squads.

In early 1989 the Inter-American Commission called for increased freedom of press, demanding that all news media be permitted to publish and broadcast without government interference. It demanded that the government guarantee "complete and unrestricted exercise of freedom of expression, right to assembly, judicial guarantees, and personal liberties."[40]

Although Amnesty International and the Inter-American Commission focused on violations by the PDF, the Popular Coordinator of Human Rights in Panama (CONADEHUPA) put its denunciations of human rights violations in terms of national sovereignty. It charged, for example, that unemployment, health care, and other measures of living standards declined as a direct result of U.S. economic aggression.

In a January 1989 report, Human Rights Watch and the Lawyers Committee for Human Rights charged that the Reagan administration "appeared to be less than a forceful advocate of human rights and democratization in Panama." The report stated:

> By throwing its support behind deposed President Delvalle, who served for years as a Noriega puppet, the Administration further underlined how superficial a house-cleaning it sought....Having

presided over repression of the protest movement that sprang to life in 1987, Delvalle can hardly be considered a standard-bearer of democracy.

Referring to the U.S. government's failure to condemn Panama for the 1984 electoral fraud and the subsequent promotion in 1985 of Delvalle as president, the human rights report observed:

The reason for this intolerance of General Noriega's presidential shuffling appears to have been the tremendous value the Administration placed on his services in running guns for and secretly training the Nicaraguan contras, in providing intelligence, in offering safe haven to an occasional deposed dictator, and in laundering funds for enterprises that were supposed to be kept off the books. So precious was this relationship that when the Panamanian military committed its most heinous crime (the 1985 abduction, torture, and decapitation of Noriega opponent Dr. Hugo Spadafora) the Central Intelligence Agency station chief in Costa Rica reportedly aided in the cover-up of the crime by providing a false witness (hired by the CIA) who appeared on Panamanian television blaming the crime on the Salvadoran guerrillas.[41]

While the human rights abuses of political dissidents have largely been limited to arbitrary arrests, harassment, and beatings, many members of the security forces who participated in the failed October 1989 coup were executed. In the aftermath of the invasion, there were mounting charges that the new government and the U.S. military were violating the human rights of those suspected of having supported the Noriega government.

Chapter 2

Military

Security Forces

With the December 1989 invasion, the U.S. military resumed its historic role as the chief arbiter and guarantor of political power in Panama. The Panama Defense Forces (PDF) and the country's civil defense put up heavier resistance than anticipated but within a few days were brought under U.S. control. Over 300 PDF members were killed in the invasion.

Suddenly, after 21 years in which the military had served as the country's central institution, the PDF ceased to exist. It was replaced at least temporarily by a new police organization labeled the Panamanian Public Force (PPF). In early 1990, under the supervision of the U.S. occupation army, the newly constituted security force, composed mainly of former PDF members, was in the process of gradually assuming control of some of the country's police functions. Widespread distrust of former PDF members who made up the PPF, the disinclination of former army officers to do police work, and a post-invasion crime wave were among the many problems faced by the new security force.

Most Panamanians were glad to be rid of the PDF which had grown increasingly repressive and corrupt. But the dissolution of the PDF left a serious gap of authority in the country. As the country began its reconstruction efforts, it faced the challenge of creating a sovereign and ordered country without resorting to U.S. troops. There was also the question of the future of the Panama Canal now that the country was unable to protect the canal with its own forces. In the shaping of the new Panama, Panamanians will have to come to terms with what the PDF was and what kind of military and police force should emerge from its ashes. Like the PDF itself, the new security forces will be largely a creation of the United States, on which it will likely depend for most of its training and supplies.

The PDF: The Army That Once Was

The PDF was born of a 1983 restructuring of the country's police and military forces. Until this restructuring, the National Guard was the country's only armed force and had both police and military functions. Prior to the U.S. invasion, all the country's military and police forces were subject to the authority of the PDF's commander-in-chief. Subordinated to the commander-in-chief were members of the general staff (*estado mayor*), whose members included the chief-of-staff, deputy chief of the Air Force, and deputy chief of Ground Forces.[1] Similar to the U.S. Army, the PDF's general staff included five divisions: Personnel, Intelligence, Operations, Logistics, and Civic Action.

The PDF had four military branches, the largest of which was the 15,000-member army or National Guard.[2] The Navy functioned more like a coast guard, while the Air Force was practically non-existent, consisting of a few helicopters and small aircraft. The fourth branch, the Panama Canal Defense Force, was actually part of the army. The PDF's police forces included the Police Force, National Traffic Directorate, National Department of Investigations (DENI), and the Immigration Department.

The country's 12 military zones corresponded to the country's provincial divisions, although Panama City had three military zones. There was also a military zone in the San Blas Indian *comarca* (reserve). Different combat or internal security units were based at the different military zones. The PDF had eight infantry companies, sometimes referred to as combat companies and bearing such nicknames as the Tigers, Red Devils, Cholos, and Pumas. The Machos del Monte expeditionary company was based at the Río Hato base on the Pacific coast. Other special units included the Public Order Company (Dobermans) and the Presidential Guard.[3] After the 1983 restructuring, two new combat battalions – Battalion 2000 (established to defend the canal) and the Battalion Peace (headquartered in Chiriquí) – were created to prepare the country for the year 2000 when Panama assumes complete control of canal and national defense.

Expanding Political and Military Role

The military and police forces of Panama long operated under the tutelage of Washington. In fact, the U.S. government was instrumental in the creation of the National Guard and was until 1987 the main source of funding and training for Panamanian police and military forces. The United States disbanded the country's small army in 1904 and its police force some ten years later, taking control over the internal and external security matters until the mid-1930s, when the end to the U.S. protectorate status was negotiated.[4]

During World War II the national police were militarized by the United States. In 1953, the year that former police chief José Antonio Remón Cantera became Panama's president, the National Police force was modernized and the National Guard created. As part of its new effort to foster hemispheric security, the Pentagon started to train and aid the country's National Guard while establishing a strong foundation of counterinsurgency and national security doctrine among its ranks.[5] In the 1960s U.S. military and economic aid programs increased under the Alliance for Progress program.

With the political parties in disarray and no plan for economic modernization in sight, Col. Omar Torrijos Herrera toppled the Arias government in 1968 and established a populist military dictatorship. The Torrijos coup made the National Guard the country's main political institution. Torrijos broke all links of oligarchic control of the National Guard and proceeded to make it the country's sponsor and protector of populist reforms — ranging from agrarian reform to the institution of a progressive Labor Code.[6] Torrijos also promoted the National Guard as the guardian of nationalist values. He demanded that the U.S. military evacuate a base in the Coclé province and led the drive to update and revise the canal treaties.

Another distinctive change in the National Guard under Torrijos was its new openness to blacks and other minorities. By giving ethnic minorities, especially blacks, increased access to the ranks and officer corps of the National Guard, Torrijos ensured widespread support among those sectors for his populist dictatorship.

From 1968 until his death in 1981, Torrijos served as the country's commander-in-chief. Col. Florencio Flores assumed that position in 1981 followed by Gen. Rubén Darío Paredes. When Paredes stepped down to run for president in 1983, Gen. Manuel Antonio Noriega became commander-in-chief. A month after he assumed that position, the National Guard was restructured under Law 20 into its current divisions. Aside from modernizing the structure of the police and military forces, Law 20 also instituted PDF control over many aspects of Panamanian public life, including the immigration department, civil aeronautics administration, railroads, traffic department, and the passport bureau.[7]

In 1987, the year that Noriega finally fell out of favor with the United States, Washington began encouraging dissident factions within the PDF to oust Noriega. Abortive coup attempts in March 1988 and October 1989 seriously depleted the PDF's officer corps, which had also been weakened by the forced retirement of many high officers suspected of harboring anti-Noriega sympathies.

Because there has been no military academy in Panama, officer candidates received their training outside the country. Some like Noriega himself were schooled in Peru or in other Latin American countries, including El Salvador and Somoza's Nicaragua. Others received instruction through U.S. military training programs at the School of the Americas in the Canal Zone and after 1984 in Ft. Benning, Georgia. At the time of the school's relocation to Georgia, Panama was the third-largest user of it in terms of total number of graduates since the school's founding in 1946.[8] Other U.S. military training was continued until 1987 at the Panama Canal Area Military Schools. (See U.S. Military Aid) The School of the Americas was occupied by the PDF's José Domingo Espinar training center. Although the country still did not have its own officer training school, it did operate the Tomás Herrera Institute, a secondary school. Most PDF officers, however, received no formal officer training.

It was the nationalist and reformist legacy of *torrijismo* that gave the PDF its credibility and sense of purpose. At the same time, however, the PDF was a largely corrupt institution that often put itself above law, morality, and government. Payoffs by businesses for special treatment were commonplace, it raked in large sums in multinational business deals, and skimmed off profits from the international drug trade and arms smuggling. The PDF also had direct economic interests, a national bank created in 1989. The PDF described the bank as a "private entity" that functioned as a branch of the Defense Forces Benevolent Society.

Planning a Barracks Mutiny

Recognizing the central place the PDF played in Panama, Washington in mid-1987 began encouraging dissident elements within the PDF to mount a coup to oust Noriega. George Shultz, secretary of state during the Reagan administration, called the PDF "a strong and honorable force that has a significant role to play, and we want to see it play that." The Bush administration also placed its hopes for the ouster of Noriega on Noriega's own troops. Following the May 1989 elections, U.S. ambassador Arthur Davis and the White house called on the PDF to remove Noriega.

After a March 1988 coup attempt by senior high-ranking officers, Noriega cleaned house, retiring other officers and strengthening links with other middle- and high-level officers. The United States apparently was hoping that anti-Noriega revelations by former chief of staff Col. Roberto Díaz Herrera, combined with clandestine coup organizing, would spur the removal of Noriega. But that effort again failed, with some suggesting that the public campaign by Herrera had actually blown the conspirators' cover. Another more serious coup attempt was launched on October 3, 1989 by mid-level officers led by Major Moisés Giroldi, but was effectively crushed by Noriega and loyal forces. It was later reported that there may have been two coup attempts underway—one led by mid-level officers and the other by a faction of military intelligence.[10] Officially, 77 died in that unsuccessful coup attempt. The ad-hoc group Pro-Liberation Committee for Detained Military Personnel claimed the numbers of killed and arrested were much higher than reported by the PDF. Following the invasion those held in military prisons were released.

Paramilitary Groups

Panama has not been plagued by the same kind of death squad terrorism seen in Guatemala, Honduras, and El Salvador. The ideological alliances and working relationships between the security forces and the right wing that have produced death squads in other Central American countries do not exist in Panama. Within the PDF, however, there have existed special units like the F-7, which is believed to have been responsible for anti-opposition violence during the 1984 election campaign. The successor to F-7, the F-8 terror squad, has been widely accused of the death squad-like killing of rightist opposition figure Hugo Spadafora and the beating of Mauro Zuñiga, head of the Coordinating Board for National Civilian Organization.[11]

In 1987 military harassment and repression of the political opposition increased. The Dignity Battalions, formed in 1988 as military-sponsored civil defense units to defend the country against U.S. intervention, were partly responsible for the harassment and beatings of the opposition movement. These voluntary paramilitary units were trained by retired PDF officers and were often accompanied by active-duty military officers. The Committees for the Defense of the Country and Dignity (CODEPADI) were also formed by the military. These were groups of civil servants in each government institution who were trained and armed for defense.

During the May 1989 election violence, it was reported that PDF members changed their uniforms for the T-shirts of the Dignity Battalions. The Strategic Military Council (CEM), created by Noriega as a parallel high command, was widely believed to have played a major role in coordinating paramilitary violence against the Civic Crusade.[12] The U.S. invasion met only spotted resistance from the country's demoralized civil defense units.

Chapter 3

Economy

The State of the Economy

Panama began the 1990s with an economy badly shaken by U.S. economic sanctions (1987-1989) and smarting from the devastation and looting that accompanied the December 1989 invasion. The gross national product had dropped dramatically—about 25 percent since mid-1987. Per capita income had been pushed back to the levels of the early 1980s. Government revenues were down about 44 percent—which had caused a similar drop in public services and investment. Industrial output had dropped by 40 percent, and the tourism sector was down to 25 percent of capacity.

With credit so scarce, the construction industry had ground to a standstill. Foreign-exchange revenues were down 50 percent, and debt payments had been suspended by the Noriega government. Official unemployment in early 1990 was at 16 percent but most observers set the real figure at 25 percent with another 25 percent being underemployed. Because of the crisis severe poverty had increased from 33 to 40 percent of the population by early 1990.[1]

Yet even before the onset of anti-Noriega campaign the Panamanian economy had been reeling from a long-festering structural crisis. The chief symptoms of structural crisis were the following: declining private and public investment, an unpayable foreign debt, decline in the international banking center, budget deficits, cutbacks in government services, decreased per capita food production, and stalled economic growth.

Rabiblancos and the Transit Economy

Historically the Panamanian economy and its business elite have been largely based on commerce and services associated with Panama Canal. The country's oligarchy—known as *rabiblancos*—have also traditionally been closely tied to the United States.

A rural elite, based on expansive cattle ranches and agricultural estates, has also existed in Panama. But this landed class has never stood at
the center of the country's economic and political power structures—in
sharp contrast to the dominant position held by the agroexport elite elsewhere in Central America.[2] For all their power and privilege, the *rabiblancos* have exercised their economic and political influence in the shadow
of such externally controlled forces such as the canal, the U.S. Southern
Command, and the international financial center.

Being at the center of world trade, Panama had long relied on imported food and manufactured goods to meet its internal needs. It was
not until after World War II that local investors began placing their accumulated capital into industrial and agroindustrial projects.[3] Panama
adopted an import-substitution model of development that fueled impressive new private investment by local capitalists and foreign corporations. Although the new industrialization did put an array of locally
produced goods on store shelves, it did nothing to broaden the market of
consumers who could afford these products.

In the 1950s and 1960s, a time when the economy was expanding at
unprecedented rates, most Panamanians continued to live and work in
misery. Increasing landlessness and rural-urban migration were just one
sign of the structural weakness and injustice of the Panamanian
economy.[4] The country lacked an economic modernization plan and a
political system that incorporated the middle and lower classes into the
governing process. With the oligarchy floundering and divided, the National Guard in 1968 moved to take the country's economic and political
agenda into its own hands.

Military-Led Reformism and Rising Debt

Torrijos and the National Guard set Panama on a new path of
economic development. Breaking the stranglehold of the oligarchy, the
Torrijos regime adopted a populist approach to economic development.
Through a series of reforms, Torrijos brought peasants and workers into
an alliance with the state and the private sector whose goal was capitalist
modernization.

A reinforced agrarian reform, a new Labor Code, and the incorporation of formerly neglected sectors into the government were among the
steps taken by Torrijos to broaden the benefits of economic development
and to expand the domestic market. Rejecting the politics of class con-
frontation, Torrijos called his populist program a "revolution of growing
aspirations" of the lower classes.[5]

Populist reforms established a stable social base. From this base, the Torrijos regime launched an economic modernization project that included public-sector productive investments (sugar, tourism, credit, etc.), infrastructure construction (hydroelectric dams, ports, and roads), the promotion of the new international finance center, and a renovation of the transnational service sector. From the beginning, the economic project of the Torrijos regime met opposition from the hidebound oligarchy. But in its effort to consolidate the internal market and to broaden the country's role as a transnational service platform, the modernization project did succeed in forging a new private-sector elite that was closely allied with the state. The quick success of the international finance center gave rise to a dominant new economic elite that was closely tied to the financial center and international capital.[6]

Torrijos was by no means a leftist revolutionary. He did shake up the country's economy and politics, but it was never his aim to displace the private sector from its central role in production and distribution. The general espoused the politics and economics of class collaboration. Always careful not to alienate the oligarchy, Torrijos tried to negotiate a middle way, a third path. "Neither with the left, nor with the right, but with Panama" was his favorite posture when faced with tense social situations.[7] As George Priestley noted, "Nonconfrontation and class cooperation were the watchwords, even in the face of resentment on the part of the groups concerned."[8]

When the National Guard took power in 1968, the economy was sailing along at an 8 percent rate of annual growth. World recession and rising oil prices were among the main factors causing this fast economic pace to slow down by 1974. The private sector, however, blamed the downturn on the populist bent of the Torrijos regime, and began its campaign to rein in *torrijismo* and establish its preeminence in the ruling alliance. As a result of this pressure and Torrijos' own efforts to draw the oligarchy into the campaign to revise the canal treaties, the weight of the government shifted markedly away from the popular sectors by the mid-1970s. The CONAC peasant confederation was defunded in 1974 (See Agriculture); the focus of agrarian policies moved from distribution to production; the Labor Code was revised (See Labor); and the regime backed away from its earlier promises to incorporate popular sectors into national policymaking.

During the 1970s the government did, however, maintain its commitment to expanding government social services, especially health and education. It also continued to insist that a large public investment budget was necessary for a expanding economy. By the turn of the decade, even these remaining elements of *torrijismo* began to shrink in the face of an incipient coalition of the country's dominant economic forces with multilateral banks, foreign private banks, and the U.S. Agency for International Development (AID). A second jump in oil prices, another downturn in world trade, and the advent of the debt crisis combined to cause the collapse of the Torrijos development model.

Rising interest rates in the late 1970s precipitated the economic crisis of the 1980s. Government social services and its direct participation in the economy through more than three dozen state enterprises had been pushed forward in large part to strengthen the internal market. It had been financed not through progressive taxation but from funds borrowed from international banks. The borrowing spree of the 1970s, encouraged by foreign private banks, resulted in the country having Latin America's largest per capita debt. In 1979 the International Monetary Fund (IMF) said that Panama had arrived "at a relationship between indebtedness and national income unprecedented in the Western Hemisphere."

By 1981 Panama could no longer keep up with the interest payments on its debt let alone pay off the principal. This crisis in international accounts was paralleled by one in the government's own budget. Falling revenues and the burden of a large government payroll and social service sector had caused the budget deficit to widen to crisis proportions.

Structural Adjustment and Neoliberalism

During the 1980s the military government attempted to tackle the structural crisis with adjustment programs imposed by the World Bank and International Monetary Fund (IMF) and backed by the Inter-American Development Bank (IDB) and the U.S. Agency for International Development (AID). The structural-adjustment measures were an attempt to reshape the country's economic model along neoliberal lines by promoting exports, cutting government programs, pushing privatization, dropping protective tariffs, and liberalizing prices.

Although these programs had some success in easing the balance-of-payments crisis and closing budget deficits, they had failed to spur significant new economic growth. Debt repayments continued to drain the national treasury and this decapitalization obstructed economic recovery. The government had moved to liberalize the economy and promote exports but export growth proved disappointing. Nontraditional agroexports showed little increase, and there was no sign that the industrial sector could at any time soon demonstrate a capacity for export production.

At the same time that the new economic model was failing to meet its initial promise, additional symptoms of the country's economic crisis had surfaced during the 1980s. Per capita production of basic grains was dropping, unemployment was steadily rising, and the country's once encouraging indices of health and education were falling. The lack of adequate housing also threatened to precipitate new social unrest.

During the crisis of the late 1980s the Noriega regime suspended debt-servicing payments. These payments had previously soaked up about 40 percent of government revenues. By defaulting, Noriega was able, despite the U.S. embargo and declining tax revenues, to continue to meet most civilian and military payroll demands. But this was clearly a temporary solution to an increasingly grave financial crisis. With government revenues continuing to nose dive, the financial collapse of the Noriega regime was all but inevitable. But rather than wait any longer, Washington chose to launch a military invasion to oust Noriega, break the PDF, and install a new government in Panama.

The economic and political crisis of the late 1980s and the U.S. campaign of economic destabilization had derailed the plans and projections of the structural-adjustment program. Following the invasion and the installation of the Endara government, steps were immediately taken to put the structural-adjustment program back on track. New agreements were in the offing between the government and foreign lenders.

The War of Economic Sanctions

Starving the government of cash was the main strategy in the war of economic aggression unleashed by Reagan and escalated by Bush. A nation whose national currency is the dollar, Panama was particularly vulnerable to Washington's economic aggression. The U.S. government expected that the government of Panama would quickly collapse when it found that it was unable to pay its bills or guarantee bank deposits. The sanctions were designed to sow political discontent with the Noriega-managed government by driving the economy into a deep recession.

The U.S. economic war against Panama began in January 1986 when the National Security Council (NSC) recommended that Economic Support Funds (ESF) scheduled for Panama be transferred to Guatemala.[9] Instead of receiving the $46 million that AID had allocated, Panama in fiscal year 1987 received just $12 million — down from $33 million the year before and $74 million in 1985.[10]

In late 1987 Washington cut off all military and most economic aid to Panama. Allowed to continued were a few scholarship and training programs, aid to several local nongovernmental organizations, and regional and Washington-based funding for U.S. private organizations active in Panama. As it became clear that the Noriega regime was not going to be easily toppled, a series of escalating economic sanctions were then imposed by Congress and the White House. In addition to restricting U.S. aid to Panama, Washington prohibited joint military exercises with the Panamanian Defense Forces, terminated the U.S. sugar quota for Panama, and required that U.S. representatives vote against any proposed loans to Panama from multilateral banks.[11]

In March 1988 President Reagan rescinded Panama's preferential tariff treatment under the Generalized System of Preferences and the Caribbean Basin Economic Recovery Act. A month later Reagan imposed sanctions under the authority of the International Emergency Economic Powers Act by declaring that the Panama government represented "an unusual and extraordinary threat to the national security." The same act had been used to justify the trade embargo against Nicaragua.

In the case of Panama, a total trade embargo was not imposed because of the United States' own dependence on Panama Canal trade and because such an embargo would blatantly violate the 1977 Canal Treaties. Instead of a complete trade embargo, Washington sought to create a destabilizing cash crunch for the regime by freezing its dollar accounts and other interests in the United States and by prohibiting U.S. individuals, companies, and government agencies from making payments to the government. Escrow accounts managed by the U.S. Department of the Treasury and Department of State were set up to collect taxes and fees that normally would be paid to the Panamanian government. This included such revenues as social security taxes paid by U.S. corporations doing business in Panama and canal toll receipts.[12]

When it became obvious that U.S. companies were evading the restrictions on paying taxes and fees to the government, Washington tightened the sanctions in 1989 to close loopholes. At the same, however, Washington was forced to back down on blanket sanctions to enable U.S. government and military personnel to remain in the country. Late in the year the Bush administration again escalated the economic war by announcing that ships registered in Panama would not be permitted to dock in the United States.

Barely able to meet its payroll, the Noriega regime had no extra funds to maintain the basic infrastructure. So cash-short was the state that it could not afford the fluoride for the country's water supply. With recession setting in, investors and entrepreneurs began pulling their capital out of the country. Many established businesses closed down, and the informal sector of the self-employed swelled as thousands of newly unemployed Panamanians went into the streets to scratch out a living. Other unemployed workers began returning to to rural areas.[13]

Economic sanctions had the desired effect of pushing the economy into a tailspin. But the economy managed to stagger along — supported by the diversity of the commercial and services sector, the wages paid to 12,000 employees of U.S. government agencies, steady income from the Colón Free Zone, and the largely unaffected agricultural sector. In its destablization strategy Washington had not counted on the flexible response of Panamanians to the illiquidity crisis (increased use of checks and vouchers) nor on the government's ability to use the sanctions to build nationalist resistance.

Initially the political opposition supported the sanctions in belief that they would be only temporary. Indeed, it was the Civic Crusade which first urged Panamanians to close down their businesses and to withhold revenues. Yet as it became clear that toppling Noriega would not happen overnight, most sectors of the society and economy criticized the measures as unproductive or even counterproductive. Although it tried to distance itself from sanctions, the Civic Crusade suffered from its inevitable association with the campaign of economic destabilization. For its part, the American Chamber of Commerce complained that the sanctions had succeeded only in "slowly strangling U.S. companies, Panamanian business persons, and the middle class."[14] The popular sectors — students, workers, peasants, and community organizations — were among the hardest hit by the country's economic decline but were largely unable to forge an independent popular response to the crisis.

Because of the country's extreme dependency on the United States, the impact of economic sanctions on Panama has been especially grave when compared with other countries where sanctions have been enforced. A 1983 study published by the Institute for International Economics showed that in most cases of economic sanctions the cost to target countries as a percentage of the national product has been only a few percentage points. Of 18 cases between 1918 and 1982, only in three countries — Iran, Rhodesia, and Surinam — did the estimated damage from sanctions reach 10 percent.[15] After just one year, U.S. sanctions caused a more than 15 percent drop in Panama's economy.

Internationally Washington received little support for the destabilization measures which violated international law and trade agreements and were an obvious breach of the 1977 Canal Treaties. Once again the United States demonstrated its willingness to set aside international rules of conduct in interests of restoring its hegemony in Central America.

Economic Crisis as Nineties Begin

Some major characteristics of the Panamanian economy as the country entered the 1990s were:

* An extremely open and dependent economy that does not even have its own Central Bank or national currency. An economy that depends on imports for most primary and personal consumption items. Wide trade imbalances have been a feature of the country's external sector since independence.

* High $2,200 per capita debt which has made the country vulnerable to harsh structural-adjustment packages. Until debt payments were canceled in 1987, more capital was flowing out of the country in debt payments than into the country in new investment and adjustment capital.

* Austerity measures and a structural-adjustment program that have pushed forward a highly questionable economic development model based on export production in a country where less than 20 percent of national income is generated by the productive agricultural and industrial sectors.[16]

* Relatively high per capita income but highly skewed income distribution. The bottom 20 percent of the population receive only 2.1 percent of national income, while the top 5 percent receive 17.8 percent.[17]

* After major advances in meeting basic needs and giving the poor access to health, education, and utilities in the 1970s, socioeconomic indicators had fallen steadily in the 1980s.

* The services and commerce sector accounts for over 50 percent of the national product but benefits from this economic activity are limited by tax and tariff exemptions.

* An economy trying to recover from a vindictive U.S. destabilization campaign that had cost the country $2 billion in reduced jobs and income and had driven Panama into recession, followed by the U.S. invasion accompanied by widespread looting that had caused at least $750 million in losses.

* In its reconstruction efforts, the new government was fortunate to count on the good will and assistance of the United States and multilateral banks — although the incoming aid fell substantially short of what the new government was requesting.

The new Endara government, while blessed with an injection of U.S. economic assistance, was hard put to restore the economy to pre-1987 levels. It faced debt payment arrears of $540 million and a devastated internal economy. Although substantial, the approximately $1 billion in promised U.S. credits and assistance fell far short of what the country really needed to restore former prosperity. Even if the debt arrears were cleared up, the country would still be confronted with one of the world's highest ratios of debt to gross national product. The debt crisis situation is aggravated by the fact that two-thirds of the country's $3.9 million public-sector debt is owed to high-interest commercial lenders. Former President Ardito Barletta estimated that for the country to return to pre-1988 levels would take 15 years.[18]

Under U.S. guidance the Endara government launched a recovery program that incorporates neoliberal economic formulas to spur growth and emergency public works programs to pacify the urban unemployed. If the country is to restore its previous economic status, recovery of the financial center will be essential. But U.S. demands to revise the bank secrecy laws that have accounted for Panama's attractiveness as an international financial center will obstruct new growth is this sector. Promoting increased export production is also a priority for the new government, which is pressed to find new sources of foreign exchange.

Cutting the budget deficit will be necessary if the government is to resume its debt payments and have access to new foreign loans. But to do that the government may be forced to lay off as many as 30,000 workers from the bloated government payroll — and thereby risk social upheaval. Privatization of state enterprises is also on the agenda, but here too the government risks sparking destabilizing protests from affected workers and citizens hit by sharp price increases.

To maintain public support for the government amid the continuing economic crisis, the Endara administration announced a cut in salaries for public officials and Endara went on a public fast for the society's poor and homeless. But more than humanitarian gestures and promises of recovery will be needed if the government is to retain public support. It must quickly prove that the U.S. invasion and private-sector remedies will lead to increased employment, rising income, and improved socioeconomic conditions.

Agriculture

Outside of the Panama City-Colón corridor, Panama is essentially an agricultural country. Together, agriculture, forestry, and fishing provide employment to 27 percent of working Panamanians — more than any other economic sector.[19] Beyond its contribution to employment, however, the agricultural sector plays a minor role in the economy, its contribution dropping from 19 percent in the late 1960s to only 9 percent of the national income with agroindustry (food processing) contributing another 4-5 percent. Agroexports account for only 28 percent of export revenues — lower than any other Central American country.

The crisis in agriculture has been particularly severe in the last ten years as export revenues declined, per capita food production fell, and food imports increased. Among the main factors for this sectoral crisis are the structural-adjustment measures that deemphasize local food production, shrinking government support for farmers, inequities in land distribution, and low crop yields.[20] Over the last three decades many rural residents have left the countryside to seek a better living in the Panama City-Colón urban corridor.

Neither terrain nor soil quality favors agriculture in Panama. Over three-quarters of the land is hilly, and only 37 percent of these hillside zones have good, deep soils — compared with 50 percent in neighboring Costa Rica or 76 percent in El Salvador.[21] Only about 30 percent of the country's land is suitable for cropping and pasture. Of this, 8 percent of the land is cultivated and 15 percent is in pasture — leaving a large agricultural frontier in Darién and other isolated regions, though most of these areas are tropical forests.[22]

Agricultural land is unevenly divided among the country's farmers, with one percent of the farms covering over 33 percent of the farm land. Over 90 percent of the farms are small holdings, representing only a third of the agricultural land. Only 4 percent of the farms are categorized as commercial, while 35 percent report no cash income at all. Clear land titles are held by just 10 percent of the country's farmers. Most of the estates larger than 500 hectares are dedicated to cattle and milk production.[23]

Slash-and-burn cultivation (known as *la roza*), machetes, and planting sticks still distinguish the agricultural practices of the small farm sector. As a result crop yields are extremely low — half the average for corn and beans production in South America.[24] Nonetheless, small and medium farmers produce most of the country's foodstuffs. The production increases that have occurred over the last couple decades have been more the result of expanding the land under production rather than improved production practices. It is only in the more organized export crops, such as bananas, sugar, and coffee, that there is substantial use of mechanization, fertilizers, and technical assistance.

The Government and the Farm Sector

In the early 1960s the government began to increase its intervention in the agricultural sector. Through Alliance for Progress programs, government technical assistance and loan programs were established. In 1963 an agrarian-reform program was established with the intent to settle landless peasants on uncultivated lands, especially in the agricultural frontier. The program, stalled by oligarchic resistance and lack of government funds, only resettled some 3,100 landless families leaving over 25,000 applications for land pending and unheeded.

The 1968 coup and the ensuing populist program of the Torrijos regime resulted in a marked increase in government attention to rural problems. Renewed attention was given to agrarian reform, government-peasant alliances were created, the rural infrastructure was expanded, and the state became a major player in agricultural production.

During the early years of the Torrijos regime, agrarian reform and other programs targeting the peasant sector were driven by both political and economic imperatives. Torrijos saw the peasantry as an important base of political support for the new government and its nationalistic foreign policy. Before Torrijos, the main political allegiances of the organized peasantry were with the communist People's Party and to a lesser extent with the nationalism and populism of Arnulfo Arias. Encouraged by the People's Party and having spent decades fighting the Chiriquí Land Company and the encroachments of the Canal Zone, there existed a strong anti-imperialist current within the peasantry. Torrijos set out to tap this anti-gringo sentiment in his own efforts to legitimize his government and assert Panamanian control over the canal. Alfredo Acuna, director of the Agrarian Reform Commission (CRA) in 1974, described the agrarian-reform process as "a means of incorporating that broad sector of the Panamanian population into the patriotic struggle for the liberation of our people."[25]

As a way of realizing this political goal of the agrarian reform, Torrijos opened up his government to the People's Party and its peasant leaders. At first distrustful of the National Guard junta that replaced the Arias presidency and unleashed a new round of repression, peasant leaders later gained more confidence in the new regime with the removal of the avowed anticommunist Col. Boris Martínez and the new populist leadership of Torrijos.[26] Recognizing that the Torrijos regime was reaching out to conservative and capitalist elements of society as well as progressive ones, the Peoples' Party entered the government with the hope that its influence would make the progressive elements dominant. In return for its support of the Torrijos regime, the peasant leadership of the Peoples' Party was given control of the National Confederation of Peasant Settlements (CONAC), established in 1970.

Unlike the Peoples' Party, Torrijos did not regard the agrarian-reform process as a challenge to traditional economic structures in rural Panama but simply as a way to increase food production while tapping underutilized land and labor. The emphasis was not expropriation of large private landholdings but distribution of unused estates and marginal lands through government auctions and land sales. Landowners were encouraged to substitute land for taxes or to accept government bonds in exchange for portions of their estates. To pacify peasant demands, the Chiriquí Land Company in the early 1970s lopped off several thousand acres of its vast enclave for the agrarian reform and later sold unused lands to the government and private purchasers.

By the mid-1970s the agrarian reform had slowed to a crawl. Large and medium-size producers complained that government funds would be better spent on more productive and commercially viable agricultural sectors. Under increasing pressure from the oligarchy, the government dropped its earlier commitment to land distribution and increasingly stressed productive investment. Without the full commitment of the government, the agrarian-reform sector found itself wallowing in debt and without adequate technical assistance and credit.

The newly established Ministry of Agricultural Development (MIDA) and the Ministry of Planning and Economic Development bypassed the peasant-controlled CONAC. Political clientelism, a torpid bureaucracy, and increased emphasis on commercial agriculture combined to undermine the agrarian-reform process and the government's commitment to the peasant settlements. By 1972 the pace of government land acquisition was already slowing down even though only 5,000 families on 200 land settlements (*asentamientos rurales*) had at that point benefited from the reform process.[27] This fell far short of the actual need and earlier government promises for extensive reform. The much touted agrarian reform of the Torrijos regime was no more effective than the program of the early 1960s, covering only 4 percent of the country's agricultural land, most of which was the most marginal land.[28]

A much stronger element in the rural program of the Torrijos regime was its commitment to extending rural infrastructure and building a dynamic state-owned farm sector. During the 1970s the government sponsored a construction boom of roads and bridges, hydroelectric plants, and rural electrification projects. The most dramatic state intervention occurred in the sugar industry with the creation of the giant La Victoria corporation. But without parallel advances in agricultural productivity and technical assistance, the agricultural sector did not experience the predicted boom.

Widening government deficits, rising foreign debt, and the resulting structural-adjustment measures of the 1980s brought the Torrijos-era agricultural policies to an end. In return for support from AID and the World Bank, the government agreed to eliminate its direct role in the agricultural sector, to promote agroexports, to rely on the free market to determine commodity prices, and to embrace the economic dictates of comparative advantage. The inclusion of the Agricultural Incentives policy as part of the three-in-one law of March 1986 represented another move away from earlier peasant-oriented agricultural policies. Although the agricultural sector is certainly in need of serious reform to promote increase productivity, it remains to be seen if the free-market policies of the 1980s lift the sector out of its stagnation.

Traditional and Nontraditional Agroexports

Bananas have long been the country's leading export, and continue to provide a steady source of foreign exchange to the beleaguered economy. In 1986 banana production earned 20 percent of the country's foreign exchange from the exports of goods. The Chiriquí Land Company, owned by United Brands, is the country's largest banana producer and exporter.

United Brands began carving out its Panamanian enclave in the early years of this century. By 1976 it owned over 200,000 acres. As part of the agrarian reform of the Torrijos era, the banana giant divested itself of most its estates, leaving it with 35,000 acres today. This opened up room for increased private and government banana production. Currently, the share of national production held by individual private producers is about 25 percent and that of the state-owned Atlantic Banana Corporation is 5 percent.[29] In addition to the Chiriquí Land Company, United Brands also owns the Fruit Processing Company and Polymer, which manufactures plastic products.

The second-largest agroexport business is the seafood (mainly shrimp) industry, in which Ralston-Purina is the major investor. Panama became a major sugar-exporting nation in 1973 as a result of major government investment in the industry. At the center of the sugar industry is the state-owned La Victoria corporation, which until the recent privatization initiative operated three sugar mills. Just at the time when the country's sugar export business was peaking, world prices began their sharp decline. The increasing substitution of corn sweeteners for cane sugar also deflated Panamanian sugar exports. The renewal of the U.S.

sugar quota—suspended in 1988 and 1989—will help shore up the sagging sugar industry, which is notoriously inefficient and uncompetitive.[30]

As part of the structural-adjustment program sponsored by AID and international lending institutions, new emphasis was placed on agroexport production in the 1980s. Before suspending assistance in 1987, AID promoted increased export-oriented production of beef, fruit, and winter vegetables. With the renewal of U.S. economic aid, this development focus is now expected to be reinstituted. One private company that benefited from U.S. aid programs was Panama Agro Export, which exported cantaloupe, watermelon, and cucumber to the United States.

New U.S. credits and the probable incorporation of Panama into the Caribbean Basin Initiative (CBI) export-promotion program, as well as direct AID support for nontraditional production, will likely lead to increased nontraditional exports. But relatively high wage and worker benefit rates, uncompetitive transportation and shipping costs, and a lack of experience will hinder rapid growth in this sector. Even if the country does experience a spurt in nontraditional export production, these products will still compose only a small part of the country's export base. The prospects of significant increases in traditional agroexport production also appear dim.[31]

Services, Industry, and Finance

Well before the opening of the canal in 1914, Panama was one of the world's major crossroads. Since the earliest days of the Spanish Main, the Caribbean coast of Panama has been a world trading center. Gold from the Inca empire was transported overland to the fairs of Portobelo near the present city of Colón on the way to the Spanish monarchy.[32] In the mid-19th century, the Panama Railroad secured the territory's status as an international crossroads. In 1903, at the same time that Panama declared its independence, it also adopted the motto *Pro Mundi Beneficio* (For the World's Benefit). Unlike other Central American countries where the politics and economies have been dominated by a rural oligarchy, the Panamanian oligarchy has been largely based in services and commerce.

Colón Free Zone Booms

At first, this service economy revolved almost exclusively around the Panama Canal. The increased canal traffic during World War II spurred further development of Panama as a transnational services platform. In

1948 the Colón Free Zone opened, established in part to stave off the post-war depression in Colón. Today, it is the second largest free zone in the world after Hong Kong. Over 500 companies employ some 5,000 people in warehousing, regional distribution, manufacturing, and wholesale trade. The targeted market for these freeport operations is Latin America and the Caribbean. Companies from Japan, Taiwan, United States, and Hong Kong are the main users of the zone. Business activity in the free zone peaked in 1981 and slumped until 1985, but it has been building ever since, reaching new heights in 1988 and 1989 despite the political crisis.

Companies locating in the free zone do not pay import duties or taxes and are not even required to secure a business license. They simply need to guarantee employment to at least ten Panamanians for the privilege of opening up business operations in one of the hundreds of pre-fab warehouses that line the free zone. This enclave of international trade, separated by high barbed-wire fence from the depressed city of Colón, accounts for 3 percent of the country's gross product.[33]

International Finance Center

Avenida Central stretches from the colonial downtown district of Casco Vieja through the bustling retail district of discount stores and sidewalk sales to Panama City's shimmering Gold Coast section where it merges with Vía España. Here is a city of towering glass skyscrapers, posh hotels, and banks from around the globe. The world's main financial centers are in London, New York, Zurich and Tokyo. What one finds along Vía España is what financial wizards call an "artificial" banking center of offshore financial institutions through which the world's financiers and traders to avoid taxes and illicit profits are easily laundered and passed into other accounts. Transnational companies also use the center to finance their international operations.

Bank secrecy had been Panamanian law since 1959, but it was the 1970 banking law that created the ideal conditions for an international offshore financial center. Besides allowing numbered accounts, the 1970 law stipulated that bank deposits were not to be taxed, that no reserves were to be required, and that profits would be exempted from local income tax. The other essential element in building the international finance center in Panama was the U.S. dollar being the country's unit of exchange. A dollar-based economy means that there is no danger of currency devaluation and the inflation rate matches that of the United States.

The international finance center was thriving by the early 1980s with over $35 billion in assets, but little of the profit from this banking complex stays in Panama. Because the offshore transactions are not taxed, the employment of more than 7,000 Panamanians is the main benefit of the finance center. There are also many indirect benefits resulting from the presence of so many offshore banks. The Panamanian Tourist Industry estimated that one in every four airport arrivals was related to the banking business.[34]

The debt crisis, the opening up of offshore centers in Miami and other places, and assaults on the country's bank secrecy conditions by U.S. tax and drug enforcement agents combined to stifle the center's growth since 1982. When the crisis broke out in 1987, the center hosted over 120 banks with $22 billion in assets and several dozen reinsurance companies with over $175 million in premiums.

Although shaken by the crisis, most banks stayed in Panama with only a few major banks like First Chicago Bank and Bankers Trust of New York closing down operations. Bank of America transferred its offshore operations to California while American Express Bank moved most its offshore financial activity to the Cayman Islands. Both banks, however, kept open their general banking business in Panama.

In early 1990 Panama was hosting 110 banks with about $15 billion in deposits.[35] The financial center will not recover, however, until "confidence" returns and the new rules of the game become clear. The chief obstacle to regaining this confidence is the U.S. pressure to rescind strict bank secrecy laws which now keep the owners of the accounts out of the reach of U.S. Drug Enforcement and Internal Revenue Service Agents.

The National Banking Commission denies U.S. charges that the laundering of drug money is central to the international finance center, noting that access to numbered accounts is attractive to a wide variety of financiers and investors.[36] The U.S. pressure to loosen the bank secrecy statutes is not the only threat to the financial center. Changing trends in world finance and the opening up of new offshore centers also continue to obstruct growth of the banking center. Nonetheless, it probably will remain, at least over the short term, a centerpiece in the Panamanian economy.

Paper Companies, Ship Registry, and a Pipeline

The registry of "paper" companies is another branch of the offshore industry found in Panama. The flexibility and ease of country's 1927 incorporation law, based on that of the State of Delaware, has resulted in an estimated 100,000 company incorporations in Panama. Before the crisis, new companies were registering at the rate of 114 a day.[37] Corporation registry in Panama facilitates bookkeeping sleights of hand that enable companies and individuals to avoid taxation in their countries of operation.

The easy incorporation law also explains why so many merchant ships fly the Panamanian flag. Panama holds second place after Liberia in the "open" registry of the world's merchant fleet (known previously as flags of convenience). A surge in the registry of Japanese ships in the early 1980s put Panama in direct competition with Liberia. Some 12,000 ships — about 10 percent of the world's merchant ships — are registered in Panama.[38]

The most recent addition to Panama's transnational service economy is the oil transshipment facility of the Panama Petroterminal company. This joint venture — 60 percent owned by U.S. investors and 40 by the Panamanian government — was formed in 1977 to assist the cross-isthmus transport of Alaska's North Slope oil.[39] The problem was that the super-tankers carrying the oil could not fit through the canal locks. As a temporary solution, the new company arranged the transfer of the oil to smaller ships that could squeeze through the canal. The permanent solution was complete in 1982 — a trans-isthmian pipeline extending from Charco Azul on the Pacific (near Puerto Armuelles) to Chiriquí's Grande Bay on the Atlantic side of the country.

Pipeline operations have been little affected by the political crisis and U.S. economic sanctions. Employing about 400 workers, it contributes 3 percent of Panama's gross national income.[40] About one-third of Alaska's North Slope annual oil production flows through the pipeline. The completion of a transcontinental pipeline in the United States will eventually reduce the amount of oil (currently about 325,000 barrels per day, down from 575,000 barrels daily) pumped across the isthmus, as will the increase in consumption and new refining facilities in the United States.

The pipeline was pushed through despite objections of local residents and environmentalists. But the company insisted that environmental considerations were given top priority in the construction of the pipeline. Nonetheless, the pipeline, which is buried three feet below the earth, rivers, and lakes it traverses, remains a pressing ecological concern. Oil spills at the two terminals represent an environmental hazard and have caused damage to endangered turtle breeding grounds.[41]

The Business of the Canal

The Panama Canal, the foundation of the transnational services platform, is the source of the country's most important transshipment business. About 5 percent of all ocean-going trade passes through the canal, with over 70 percent of it originating in or destined for the United States.

Every day 30 or more ships slowly make their way through the canal, paying high fees for the privilege of not having to make the long trip down and around Cape Horn. The average toll paid is $26,000 but the fees range as high as $107,000 paid by the Queen Elizabeth II luxury liner in early 1988.

The Panama Canal Commission, which administers the canal, employs more than 1,000 U.S. citizens and 6,000 Panamanians. Over 8 percent of the country's national product comes from the canal operations. Although canal traffic reached new peaks in the 1980s, its days as an essential link in world trade seem numbered unless it is upgraded and widened. Studies have also suggested the creation of a sea-level canal (one without locks), but the $35 billion needed for such an undertaking make it unlikely. All of the three main possibilities for upgrading the canal — widening the Culebra Cut, creating a third set of locks, and building a sea-level canal — have been put on hold because of U.S.-Panama tensions. The treaty stipulation that the canal has to be handed over to Panama "free of liens and debts" presents another obstacle to U.S. investment in canal improvement during the 1990s.

Another canal modernization idea is the creation of a container transshipment center that would exchange container cargo between main shipping lines that pass through the canal. The Centropuerto project, approved by the government, was stalled because of the economic and political crisis of the late 1980s. Although the project would certainly create a new source of government revenues, the modernization scheme would likely entail the privatization of the port authority and the dismissal of numerous port workers.[42]

Because five of the nine members of the Panama Canal Commission's board of directors are appointed by Washington, decision-making about canal operations has remained largely in U.S. hands. In late 1989 U.S.-Panama tensions centered around the appointment of a new commission administrator. According to the provisions of the 1977 Canal Treaties, this post would be transferred on January 1, 1990 from a U.S. citizen to a Panamanian named by the Panamanian government and confirmed by the United States. President Bush rejected the nomination of newspaper publisher Tomás Altamirano Duque by the Noriega-controlled National Assembly on the grounds that Noriega's government was illegitimate and not recognized by the United States. Instead, Bush proposed the appointment of deputy administrator, Panamanian Fernando Manfredo. After the invasion, Manfredo was appointed for a six-month period after which time the new government was to select its own nominee.

Domestic Industry

Being an international crossroads, Panama has never developed a strong industrial sector of its own. Manufacturing and mining currently represent less than 9 percent of the gross national product and employ about the same percentage of the workforce.

It was not until after World World II that a local manufacturing sector began to emerge in Panama, mostly in the food-processing industries. Between 1946 and 1956 manufacturing expanded faster than any other economic sector.[43] Import-substitution policies, which encouraged local manufacturing growth with protective tariffs and import quotas, sparked another spurt of industrial growth in the 1960s.[44] The country's small domestic market and its lack of access to the Central American Common Market have, however, limited the growth and efficiency of the local industrial sector.[45] Today, the main components of Panama's manufacturing sector are food and beverage processing, textiles, petroleum products, chemicals, and construction materials.

During the 1980s the sector experienced negative growth. As part of the structural-adjustment program imposed on Panama by international financial institutions and AID, tariff and quota barriers protecting the small manufacturing sector were removed and industries were encouraged to move to export-oriented production. In March 1986 the government set in place a tariff reduction schedule. At the same time, the Labor Code was revised to loosen restrictions on productivity premiums, piece work, and contract work in homes — measures designed to spur new investment in export-oriented manufacturing.

The relatively high labor and infrastructure (energy and transportation) costs of doing business in Panama limit the prospects for export-oriented manufacturing in Panama. After the invasion, Washington moved to once again integrate Panama into the Caribbean Basin Initiative (CBI), but expanding U.S. protectionism has largely counterbalanced the benefits from the export incentives offered by this regional program. In the late 1980s, for example, the U.S. textile industry acted to block increased imports of sweaters and other products into the U.S. market. Although U.S. export-oriented manufacturers did not invest in Panama during the 1980s, by the middle of the decade numerous Asian textile manufacturers began to establish assembly operations in Panama to take advantage of access to the U.S. market through the CBI.

Chapter 4

Society and Environment

Popular Organizing

Activism by the popular sectors of poor and working-class Panamanians dates back to the Renters' Movement of 1925, when poor urban residents demanded better and cheaper housing. These urban protests, which were closely associated with the labor movement and inspired by socialist and anarchist ideology, established a militant legacy for the country's popular movement. Especially in Panama City, the popular movement has also exhibited a strong nationalist character — as was made clear in the anticolonialist demonstrations of 1964 in the Canal Zone.[1]

Despite its long tradition of political activism, the popular sectors played a largely passive role in the political crisis of the late 1980s. At a time of rapidly worsening economic conditions and intensifying U.S. pressure, the popular sectors remained unorganized and without a political agenda. Ideological differences, leadership struggles, the lack of good popular education programs, and the absence of a unifying political program all weakened the popular movement. As sociologist Raúl Leis observed, "The popular sectors, for the most part, have not been able to establish themselves as a popular movement (the dynamic and organized part of the popular sectors)....What we find is a people without a plan for political power."[2]

Pacifying Effects of Torrijismo

Most observers attribute this lack of political dynamism and militancy of the Panamanian majority to the success of *torrijismo* in the 1970s. The 1960s were a time of rapidly expanding political (and often revolutionary) consciousness on the part of workers, students, and peasants. But during the 1970s the popular sectors lost the initiative. According to Marco Gandásegui of the University of Panama, "In the 1970s, the military regime coopted popular organizations and divided them. It was the military which now carried the banner of national sovereignty, the recovery of the Canal Zone, agrarian reform, and educational reform. Only the student movement maintained its form, but that too has now been demobilized."[3]

The Torrijos regime succeeded in pacifying and coopting most elements of the popular movement as part of its reformist effort to modernize the government and the economy. In the agrarian sector, the government sponsored colonization and land-distribution projects that targeted the most conflictive rural areas. Although only 5 percent of the peasant population benefited and the structure of land ownership remained much the same, Torrijos did manage to place a lid on rural unrest and win the support of formerly neglected peasant communities.

The new Labor Code of 1972 increased employee rights and facilitated union organizing. One result was the integration of the labor movement into the government's broader modernization project. Union activists and leaders of other popular sectors were brought into government as members of various public-sector commissions and committees — the result being the loss of their independence and militancy.

As part of its populist program, the government established hundreds of village "health committees" throughout the country. Health conditions did improve, but the government took measures to insure that local committees did not become a forum and catalyst for more independent community organizing. By establishing the new national political infrastructure of _corregimientos_ and a new National Assembly, the Torrijos regime did undermine the local power of the old _patrones_ but only to substitute it with a system of political representation controlled by the central government. The reformism of the 1970s was not directed by the popular movement. Instead, the popular sectors formed the base of support for the government's own political and economic projects.[4]

Although the reformist character of _torrijismo_ did have the effect of integrating most popular elements into the government's own stabilization plan, there also existed a more combative and independent edge to the popular movement in the 1970s. Within the Catholic church, base communities constituted an important force of social activism.

One of the most militant sectors of the popular movement has been the urban land squatters known as _precaristas_. Since the 1950s poor Panamanians have increasingly resorted to illegal land occupations. At first, _precarismo_ was limited to the Panama City area, but in the 1980s, land occupations have occurred in Colón and Chiriquí. These squatter settlements are known variously as _barriadas brujas_ (underground/unofficial areas), *barriadas de emergencia* (emergency settlements), and *asentamientos espontáneos* (spontaneous settlements). They are a response to the country's deficit of 200,000 houses.[5]

San Miguelito, a sprawling area on the outskirts of Panama City, is a product of this squatters' movement. Today, over 9 percent of the nation's population and 20 percent of Panama City residents live in this collection of *barriadas*.[6] Representing these tens of thousands of squatters is the San Miguelito Coordinator of Spontaneous Settlements, which gained legal recognition in 1986. Its members fight for land titles and for the extension of city services into their communities. Although the squatters or *precaristas* represent a major social sector in Panama, they did not formulate their own political demands in the face of the crisis of the late 1980s. The military-controlled regime tried to manipulate their political sympathies by targeting these desperately poor communities for special government community-development projects and for civic-action programs by the PDF. While the residents of San Miguelito were certainly not the driving force behind the National Civic Crusade, many did support this elitist political opposition movement, feeling that an end of hostilities between the United States and Panama would mean more jobs.

As the country's crisis intensified in the late 1980s, there were several failed attempts to revitalize the popular movement. Two such efforts have been the formation of the United Popular Front (FUP) and the Coordinator of Popular Panamanian Organizations (COPP), which brought together unions and other popular organizations to formulate a series of political and economic demands. Yet apart from proclamations and demands, there existed little other evidence of a popular movement. Different sectors continued to raise specific demands related to their own concerns, but no overall political vision arose that would encompass the broader and long-term needs of the poor majority. The popular movement lacked a unifying political platform as well as the organizing and mobilizing capacity needed to back up its demands.

In this context of immobilization and absence of an independent political project, the popular sectors were manipulated by both Noriega and the Civic Crusade/ADOC opposition. As Leis concluded, "For the government and the opposition, the popular sectors are a crowd without faces, a docile and submissive mass that serves as social base for each of their political projects."[7]

Post-Invasion Evaluation

The U.S. invasion brought a violent close to the era of military-led populism in Panama. With the installation of the Endara administration, the popular sectors and the left wing could no longer look to the government and military for support. Although the alliance between government and the popular sectors had been disintegrating since the late 1970s, the promise of *torrijismo* continued to be used by the Noriega regime to keep the popular sectors off balance and compromised. In the 1990s the popular sectors face the challenge of building an independent movement

---

The Civic Crusade

The National Civic Crusade emerged in June 1987 following the denunciations of Col. Roberto Díaz Herrera, former military chief-of-staff. The Crusade was created to give political form to the spontaneous demonstrations that erupted in the wake of Díaz Herrera's charges against Noriega. Following his dismissal, Díaz Herrera charged that Noriega conspired with the U.S. Southern Command to kill Torrijos, was responsible for the murder of anti-PDF dissident Hugo Spadafora, and that the government of the day was there by electoral fraud.

The Crusade, an umbrella group of some 200 mostly business and professional organizations, led protests and strikes against the Noriega regime.[8] But it failed to demonstrate the resolve and popular support necessary to seriously challenge the increasingly brutal Noriega government. Sponsored by wealthy businessmen and professionals disaffected by the regime, the Civic Crusade never made a serious effort to incorporate the popular sectors into the coalition. Its activists were for the most part middle-class citizens, and the organization could not overcome its *rabiblanco* image. The credibility of the Civic Crusade was also seriously undermined by its close identification with the U.S. State Department and the U.S. campaign of economic destabilization. Nevertheless, the Civic Crusade presented the only real internal opposition to the Noriega regime. The Civic Crusade dropped its original nonpartisan posture when it joined the ADOC political coalition to campaign in the May 1989 elections.

Describing the class character of the Civic Crusade, a May 1989 *New York Times* report observed: "When the regime cracked down, often brutally, many stopped taking part in the protests, sending their maids. Many would not even risk damaging their pots and pans when banging on kitchenware became an opposition symbol. Instead, they played tapes of the sound on cassette recorders. Some complained to human rights monitors when riot troops scratched the finish on protesters' luxury cars."[9]

and forging new alliances. The longtime leaders of the popular sectors and leftwing parties will be severely encumbered by their association with the Noriega regime, while emerging leaders and organizations will likely be handicapped by their lack of experience and ideology.

The widespread support in Panama for the U.S. invasion was disheartening for many Panamanian social activists and educators. Despite news reports, not all Panamanians backed the invasion. The overwhelming nature of the invasion and the subsequent house searches and arbitrary arrests of suspected Noriega sympathizers quieted the minority opposed to the U.S. intervention.

The deep disgust felt by most Panamanians for Noriega was the immediate explanation for the initial enthusiastic support for the invasion. Many Panamanians had convinced themselves, as Frederick Kempe observed, that ridding the country of Noriega was Washington's responsibility. They believed that Noriega was "America's 'Frankenstein,' and thus the gringos must destroy him."[10] For two years they had suffered through a deteriorating economy, increasing repression, growing dictatorial powers, an annulled election, and failed military coups. By late 1989 there was a broad sentiment that only Washington could save the country and enforce a democratic transition.

The military regime since 1968, and particularly during the late 1980s, had constructed a false dichotomy between democracy and nationalism. In the end, as Raúl Leis noted, nationalism was seen as the equivalent of supporting Noriega and meant identifying with a corrupt and repressive dictatorship. Noriega had robbed the historic nationalism and appropriated it to justify his personal rule. For Panamanians it became increasingly difficult to be an advocate of both nationalism and democracy.[11] According to Leis, "The opposition put democracy ahead of nationalism" and the popular movement "was blackmailed by officialist nationalism. It was a false dichotomy, because in this country we need three things: democracy, nationalism, and popular measures."

Labor and Unions

The Panamanian labor movement, like other components of the country's popular movement, was weak, badly fragmented, and without clear direction during the 1980s. Its longstanding and close ties to the military government handicapped its ability to formulate an independent and popular response to the political and economic crisis of the late 1980s. The country's economic downturn, which accelerated after 1987, caused thousands of unionized workers to lose their jobs and also contributed to a rapid decline in the strength of Panamanian unions.

Although unions grew increasingly critical of the Noriega regime, they generally stayed within the government alliance. The labor movement echoed Noriega's nationalist rhetoric without establishing a foundation for a more popularly based political alternative to the military government. As a consequence, the labor movement was exceedingly isolated and vulnerable in the wake of the U.S. invasion. With its ties to government severed and the business elite in ascendence, the labor movement was pushed back to the pre-1968 period.

Despite the labor movement's alliance with the military government, only 17 percent of the labor force was organized before the onset of the crisis.[12] As conditions worsened, the unions lost members and the numbers of unemployed and underemployed soared. By 1989 combined unemployment and underemployment estimates had risen to 50 percent.[13]

The 1990s present new challenges to the labor movement. Burdened by their past connections with the military, the unions will have to change their organizing methods and leadership if they hope to achieve the credibility they will need to defend the rights and interests of Panamanian workers. In the past, widespread corruption, compromises with undemocratic regimes, hierarchical organizations, and manipulative practices have prevented the unionized sector from assuming a strong and independent role in the popular movement. With a rightist government in place, the union movement will need all the strength it can muster to fight further revisions in the Labor Code, privatization of state enterprises, the *solidarismo* movement, and the massive layoff of state employees.

Brief History of Labor Organizing

Labor organizing and workplace struggles have also existed in modern Panamanian society, but before 1968 the labor movement always found itself at odds with the economic and political elite. Railroad workers were the first to organize and fight for better pay and conditions. In the late 1800s numerous strikes were called against the U.S.-owned railroad. The French Canal Company was also a target of strikes in 1881 and 1896, and after 1903 strikes and work stoppages also hit the U.S. canal construction effort.[14]

Canal workers organized to protest discrimination, inhuman working conditions, and poor food and housing, as well as low and racist pay scales. During the years of the canal construction, the organizing efforts were supported by churches and mutualist societies established by the largely

Caribbean workforce. Two such groups were the Colored Progressive Association and West Indian Protective League.[15]

Worker organizing by these associations culminated in a 1920 strike involving over 17,000 laborers — most of those who were being paid in silver (the management and whites were paid in gold). The Panamanian government intervened, demanding that U.S. authorities keep the strikers within the Canal Zone and then deporting 2,000 black workers.[16] A year after the famous 1920 strike the Panamanian Workers Federation was founded among others by several anarcho-syndicalists from Spain. This first labor federation soon split into two opposing political factions. The more progressive members, who had formed the Communist Group, rejected the federation's links with the AFL-CIO and in 1924 founded the General Workers Union. Members of the original Communist Group also later founded the Communist Party (known after 1943 as the People's Party) in 1930 and the Socialist Party in 1932.[17]

Although the General Workers Union was short-lived, it did play a leading role in the Renters' Strike of 1925, having organized the League of Renters. Once again the government responded with deportations and repression. To break the renters' strike, U.S. troops occupied the cities of Panama and Colón. Following the strike, all labor organizing was suppressed by the government until World War II.

Both the U.S.-linked Workers Federation and the leftist General Workers Federation disintegrated during the next 15 years. But the labor organizations that formed in the 1940s and the 1950s maintained their predecessors' ideological proclivities and the resulting factional divisions.[18] With World War II came increased canal traffic and the emergence of a domestic import-substitution industry. As the economy changed, new labor organizations formed around the various trades. These unions, organized for the most part by the socialist and communist leaders of the 1920s, joined together in 1945 to form the Panamanian Union Federation (FSTRP). Over the next quarter century, FSTRP was at the center of most of the country's labor and popular movements. (FSTRP became the CNTP in 1970.) Protests, strikes, and marches led by the FSTRP resulted in the enactment of price-control laws, renters' laws, and the country's first minimum-wage law. Representatives from the FSTRP also formed part of the Labor Code Commission, which approved the country's first Labor Code in 1947. One of the most militant elements within the FSTRP were the unions of seamstress and tailors, who were led by Marta Matamoros, a labor heroine in Panama and founding member of the FSTRP.

More than a labor federation, FSTRP took up the banner of national sovereignty in the late 1940s and moved to get the proposed Filos-Haines Canal Treaties rejected by the National Assembly. In the 1950s it protected squatters against government evictions and formed neighborhood associations in shanty towns.[19] For their dedication to popular causes, FSTRP leaders frequently became victims of police repression. President José Antonio Remón, who served as Chief of Police until he became president in 1952, outlawed communist organizations and banned the FSTRP and the progressive Federation of Panamanian Students (FEP). During the 1950s and 1960s many labor leaders were forced to work clandestinely or leave the country.[20]

In contrast to the government's treatment of FSTRP, the Panamanian Workers Federation (CTRP) formed in 1956 with the blessings of the government. This was the result of U.S. pressure on the Remón government to facilitate the creation of a U.S.-linked labor confederation to counterbalance the leftist FSTRP. Once again, the country's labor movement was split between its leftist and conservative wings. From its beginning CTRP counted on the support of the the AFL-CIO and (after 1962) the American Institute for Free Labor Development (AIFLD).

The early 1960s were marked by intense workers' struggles, particularly in the banana and sugar industries. For decades United Fruit had successfully crushed unionizing efforts with mass firings. "Rabble rousers" and their families were loaded onto company trains and abandoned in isolated regions of the Chiriquí grasslands.[21] New strikes in 1960 and 1964 gained recognition for two banana workers' unions, one linked to FSTRP and the other to CTRP.

The pre-1968 labor movement was characterized by its effort to win popular support. Subject to government repression and victimized by unfavorable labor laws, the unions knew that only with popular support could it achieve its demands. Things changed dramatically after 1968. No longer was the labor movement on the margin. Torrijos gave union leaders a preferential position in his military government. In efforts to gain legitimacy for his new regime, Torrijos turned to the labor movement, hoping to make it part of his political base much as Juan Perón had used Argentinean labor to establish one-man rule.[22]

The enactment of the pro-union Labor Code of 1972 provided more than most unions had ever hoped for. Workers were guaranteed job security after two years, union dues were collected for all workers covered by labor agreements, and the right to strike and collective bargaining was upheld. The decidedly pro-labor tone of the new code was set forth in its first article:

The present Code governs relations between capital and labor, establishing special state protection in favor of the workers, so that the state may intervene with the purpose of providing remunerative employment to all those who lack it, ensuring every worker the necessary economic conditions for a decent standard of living.[23]

The 1972 code came at a time when the oligarchy and business sector were in disarray while the union movement was gaining unprecedented power and prestige. Both of the two main labor confederations — CTRP and CNTP — enjoyed close relations with the Torrijos government.[24] Besides granting workers new rights and guarantees, the 1972 code provided for the formation of the National Council of Organized Workers (CONATO) as a consultative organization of union representatives. While the Labor Code did protect private-sector workers, public-sector employees were excluded. No corresponding Civil Service Code protected government employees, although specific legislation does govern labor relations in certain autonomous public-sector agencies.

During the 1970s the labor sector expanded rapidly, particularly the CNTP. New independent unions and federations were formed, including the Isthmian Workers Central (CIT), Authentic Independent Workers Central (CATI), Construction Workers Union (SUCTRACS), and the Panamanian Transport Workers Central (CPTT).

By the middle of the decade the private sector had regrouped and successfully pressured the government to revise the controversial 1972 Labor Code. More than any other measure, the Labor Code had served to define the Torrijos government as reformist, populist, and pro-labor. Its revision in 1976 through Law 95 promoted by CONEP and other private-sector organizations signaled a change in the political direction of the regime.

In advancing its support for Law 95, the business sector had argued that the economic downturn of the early 1970s was directly linked to the 1972 Labor Code, which they said discouraged new economic activity. While the government's approval of Law 95 was a blow to the labor movement, it did force it to reorganize and unite to fight the growing political power of the country's dominant economic forces. By 1981 the tenuously unified labor movement was able to force the government to remove the most restrictive measures of Law 95 but it never regained the privileged position it had enjoyed in the early 1970s.

Labor in the Eighties

The successful campaign to overturn Law 95 united the labor movement as never before, but after 1981 this temporary unity broke down in the face of the historic divisiveness and political maneuvering of the union federations. The weak and disunified state of the union movement was aggravated by the steady displacement of the labor and popular sectors from their former alliance with government. In the 1980s the private sector expanded its control over economic policymaking. This resulted in increased collaboration with international financial institutions like the World Bank, giving way to the politics of austerity, the privatization of state-run enterprises, and the primacy of business interests.

The union movement in the private sector grew steadily weaker in the 1980s. Government and the private sector teamed up to prevent unionization in the international service sectors like the financial center and the Colón Free Zone, thereby blocking the union movement's access to some of the more dynamic economic sectors. In March 1986 the labor movement was unable to block further anti-labor revisions in the Labor Code. Although a commission was created in 1987 to formulate a new minimum wage, the government failed to enact a higher minimum-wage level.

Labor struggles were concentrated in the public sector during the 1980s. The National Federation of Public Workers (FENASEP), created in 1984, represents over half the country's 150,000 public-sector labor force. The Coordination of State Enterprise Workers (CSEE) is a smaller association of the employees of six autonomous public-sector agencies. Not protected by the country's Labor Code, FENASEP has been fighting for the right to strike, unionize, and bargain collectively. Through protests and work stoppages, public workers slowed down the pace of privatization and blocked massive layoffs of government workers. FENASEP, like most of country's labor organizations, refused to join the Civic Crusade's campaign to topple Noriega—not because it fully supported the Noriega regime but because it felt that the greater threat to the welfare of the workforce was the destabilizing campaign of the U.S. government.

FENASEP's president Hector Alemán defended FENASEP's refusal to join either the left or right opposition to the government, saying, "We must unite with all those who agree on the objective of completing the formation of an independent national state in Panama." Without a Civil Service Code to protect government employees, FENASEP feels that a political victory by the oligarchy would precipitate massive firings of public-sector workers and would be a severe setback for the popular sectors.[25]

Joining with the National Council of Organized Workers (CONATO) and the Coordinator of Panamanian Popular Organizations (COPP), FENASEP in 1988 demanded the departure of the U.S. Southern Command, suspension of foreign debt payments, nationalization of banks, and a foreign policy independent of Washington. In the late 1980s FENASEP called numerous public protests against government corruption and patronage, austerity measures, and the militarization of government enterprises like the Electricity Institute.

When the Civic Crusade called for a general strike of workers and business owners in early 1988, unions, for the most part, refused to join. Important exceptions were the independent associations of educators and health workers. Expressing the sentiments of the leftist unions, the CNTP's Manuel Meneses said, "Despite our differences with the Noriega government, we unite with it in opposing U.S. attacks on our sovereignty." The CNTP and other union federations like FENASEP called it a strike of proprietors and businessmen, not workers.[26] By 1989 most unions had tried to distance themselves from the government but at the same time maintain a neutral posture in the face of the intensifying political crisis.

Although not yet strong, the anti-union *solidarista* movement based in Costa Rica has made some inroads in Panama. This business-sponsored movement, which aims to establish labor-management mutual benefit associations, first appeared in the Coca-Cola company of Panama.[27] With the labor movement having lost its privileged access to government, it is likely that *solidarismo* will steadily expand in the 1990s.

Major Labor Organizations

National Council of Organized Workers (CONATO): Established in 1973 in accordance with the Labor Code as a union collaborative and consultative umbrella group, CONATO has no authority over member unions and several major organizations like CPTT and CIT are not included. Since its beginning CONATO has been wracked by the same ideological divisions that divide the country's confederations. Only in regards to changes in the Labor Code was CONATO able to demonstrate a united front. In the face of the political crisis, CONATO remained neutral, defending the nation's sovereignty against the U.S. campaign, but not allying itself with either the government or the Civic Crusade. It is a largely ineffective organization with little mobilizing capability.

National Central of Panamanian Workers (CNTP): Founded in 1970 as an outgrowth of the FSTRP (founded in 1945). Leftist orientation, and affiliated internationally with the World Federations of Trade Unions (WFTU) and the Permanent Congress of Trade Union Unity of Latin America (CPUSTAL). In the region, it is affiliated with the Central American Trade Union Committee (CUSCA). Within Panama, it is linked to the People's Party. The CNTP is composed of six federations and 24 unions, and major local affiliates include National Federation of

Food, Beverage, and Tobacco Workers, Workers Union of the Telecommunications Institute (INTEL), Workers Union of the Institute for Electrification (IRHE), and National Union of Typesetters.

Panamanian Workers Federation (CRTP): Founded in 1956, CRTP is the country's largest confederation. Internationally, it is affiliated with the International Confederation of Free Trade Unions (ICFTU), Interamerican Regional Organization of Workers (ORIT), and in Central America with the Confederation of Central American Workers (CTCA). Funding and training for CRTP has come largely from the AFL-CIO and AIFLD. From 1985 through 1990, it was allocated $1.3 million by AIFLD. CRTP includes 11 federations and 65 unions, the most important of which are Local 907 (Panamanian workers in U.S. Army installations), Federation of Workers of the Central Provinces (mainly sugar workers), Industrial Federation of Food, Beverage, and Hotel Workers (FITAHBA), National Union of Bank Employees (SINABAN), and SITRACHILCO (banana workers of Chiriquí Land Company in Bocas). Since the early 1980s CRTP has made an effort to become more politically active. Until the 1987-1989 crisis CRTP was closely associated with the Democratic Revolutionary Party (PRD) and followed the government's political lead. The wealthiest confederation, CRTP has exerted considerable influence through its AIFLD-sponsored education programs. According to the AIFLD plan for CRTP activities in 1985, CRTP had to seek to "influence economic, social, and political development of Panama through effective electoral and public opinion activities....If CRTP is to have more influence, it must become more politically active."[28] Shortly before the U.S. invasion AIFLD director Bill Dougherty threatened to cut off all support unless the CRTP followed the U.S. foreign policy position and demonstrated against the Noriega regime.[29] Refusing to adopt the U.S. position, CRTP lost its monthly allotment of over $12,000 from AIFLD. The confederation's secretary general is Ricardo Monterrey, who also sits on the U.S. board of directors of AIFLD.

Panamanian Transport Workers Central (CPTT): Organized in 1974 by the government CPTT is not a member of CONATO since many of its members are considered to be self-employed and not workers. It is not affiliated to any international organizations but was closely tied to the PRD ruling party.

Isthmian Workers Central (CIT): Founded in 1959, CIT is Christian Democratic in political orientation. It is affiliated with the World Confederation of Laborers (WCL) and the Latin American Workers Central (CLAT). Its members include six federations and 25 unions, most of which are in services and commerce. Its secretary general is Julio César Pinzón.

Authentic Workers Central (CATI): Organized in 1974 after a split in CIT, it has no international affiliations. CATI has three federations and 19 unions, including the Authentic Federation of Workers (FAT), Federation of Wood and Construction Industry Workers (FETI-COMMS), and the Workers Federation of Chiriquí (FESITRACHI). A small but militant federation, it is regarded by some as Trotskyite in political orientation. The government withheld official recognition until 1981. Its secretary general is Gabriel Castillo.[30]

The majority of the more than 12,000 Panamanian employees and the several hundred U.S. citizens working in the Panama Canal Area are represented not by Panamanian labor unions but by those directly affiliated with the AFL-CIO.[31] Among those unions are American Federation of State, County, and Municipal Employees (AFSCME), American Federation of Government Employees (AFGE), and the National Maritime Union (NMU). These unions remain independent of the government. Local 907 of AFSCME is the largest of the unions in the Canal Area. Despite the political and economic crisis, labor relations in the Canal Area have remained relatively peaceful, although workers are concerned about the future of their unions after the canal is in Panamanian control.

Education and Students

As a result of a higher per capita income and due to educational reforms implemented in the 1960s and 1970s, Panamanians as a whole are more literate and have better access to educational institutions than many other Central Americans. In the mid-1980s the illiteracy rate was estimated to be 11.8 percent, with some 90 percent of the population having at least a grade-school education.[32] Recent statistics indicate that 93 percent of children between the ages 6 and 14 are attending school. Over 95 percent of primary and secondary school students successfully complete their education, although only 61 percent finish their studies in the scheduled length of time — a figure that is rising.[33]

These impressive achievements in extending education throughout the countryside have been undermined by the economic crisis and government cutbacks. Although there was a spurt of classroom building in the early 1980s, the reformism of the Torrijos years gave way to structural adjustment and by the end of the decade the government was spending a declining portion of its budget on education. From 1977 to 1987 the percentage of the national budget dedicated to education dropped from 19.8

to 10.3 percent.[34] Beginning in 1987 students were also victims of the political crisis as schools were closed by the government during strikes and states of emergency.

Panama has two national universities—the University of Panama (UP) and the Technological University of Panama (UTP)—and one private university associated with the Catholic church—University Santa María La Antigua (USMA). There is also the Panama Canal College, which is associated with the U.S. Department of Defense Dependents Schools.

Founded in 1935, UP is the country's educational center. It has also served as a center for progressive political research and activism. In its attempt to maintain high educational standards, UP requires first-year students to pass an admissions test. Recently, only 5 percent of those entering the university have successfully passed the test, requiring the failing students to take a summer preparation course. Secondary school administrators complain that the test is too difficult, while UP officials say that the primary and secondary school systems are not providing high-quality education.[35]

Beginning in the 1940s a strong student movement developed in Panama. Unlike elsewhere in Latin America, the strongest force in this movement has been secondary school and not the university students. Panamanian high school students gained their place in history with the "Flag Riots" of 1964 when 21 students were killed and 400 wounded by Canal Zone police and U.S. soldiers. The "riots" were set off when Panamanian students attempted to raise the nation's flag in front of Balboa High School in the Canal Zone.

Both high school and university students have played a leading role in pushing forward national sovereignty issues in Panama. In addition, university students were instrumental in the effort to have the government open up educational opportunities for the country's poor and rural population.

In the 1980s the student movement was largely demobilized. Among the student organizations active prior to the U.S. invasion were the anti-government Revolutionary Student Front (FER), the pro-government University Reform Front (FRU), and the Guaycuchos (student branch of the Revolutionary Workers Party).

Students were active on both sides of the pre-invasion political conflict. Ad-hoc student protest organizations like the Action Group and the Civil Student Movement formed to support the Civic Crusade and ADOC. Their protests were often brutally crushed by the military and police. Other student factions mounted protests in front of the U.S. embassy and denounced ADOC for being an instrument of the U.S. government.

Communications Media

Historically the media in Panama has seldom strayed out of the hands of the country's oligarchy. Between 1968 and 1989, however, the military regime forged its own media empire — publishing its own newspapers and shutting down media considered too critical of the military or government. Immediately after taking power in October 1968, the National Guard closed down several newspapers published by Pan American Publishing Company, which was owned by the Arias Guardia family. Two radio stations associated with Arnulfo Arias were also closed.[36]

In 1969 the new military regime established an official government radio station called Radio Libertad, which later became Radio Nacional. The following year the government expropriated the Pan American Publishing Company and changed its name to Editora Renovación (ERSA). During the 1970s the private media was closely controlled, and in 1975 the Torrijos regime closed Radio Impacto for its intense criticism of the government. With the signing of the 1977 Canal Treaties, there was increased press freedom but the regime soon clamped down again. In 1979, for example, several radio commentators were banned because of their strong anti-government opinions.

Despite pervasive government control, the independent press continued to push forward. The most important of the anti-government papers that appeared in the 1980s was *La Prensa*. Upon becoming defense minister in 1982, General Paredes stepped up the repression against the opposition media, temporarily closing down several papers, including *La Prensa*. Besides the appearance of new dailies in the early 1980s, two new television stations (channels 5 and 13) begin broadcasting, joining channels 2 and 4.

A new wave of repression of the media followed the June 1987 revelations by Col. Roberto Díaz Herrera. A state of emergency suspended freedom of the press, and the powerful Radio KW Continente was shut down by the military. As the crisis heated up, military repression of the press also intensified. In February 1989, Noriega, infuriated by all the bad publicity, again closed several radio stations and newspapers including *La Prensa*. The ouster of Noriega in December 1989 caused a flourishing of media operations. The newspapers *La Prensa*, *El Siglo*, and *El Extra* were reopened, and *Crítica* was returned to its previous owners.

Print Media

All the country's daily newspapers are published in Panama City and are poorly distributed outside the capital. The three main opposition newspapers—*La Prensa*, *El Siglo*, and *El Extra*—were closed by the Noriega regime in response to mounting anti-government opposition. The largest of these is *La Prensa*, a daily owned by Roberto Eisenmann, one of the country's most powerful businessmen.[37] *El Siglo*, founded in 1985, was a sensationalistic newspaper owned by Jaime Padilla Beliz and a group of investors. *El Extra*, owned by Gilberto Arias Guardia (former owner of *Crítica*) was a voice for the *arnulfistas* of the PPA. (See Politics)

Before the invasion, the regime's media conglomerate ERSA ran three dailies: *La República*, *Crítica*, and *Matutino*. Another pro-regime paper was *La Estrella de Panamá*, which dates back to 1849 and has consistently supported the government in power. It is owned by the Duque family, and its director is Tomás Altamirano Duque, the man Noriega appointed to administer the Panama Canal.[38] The U.S. Information Service (USIS) complained in early 1989 that *La Estrella*, which had been consistently anti-communist and pro-United States, had in the last few years become increasingly critical of the United States.[39]

Two valuable sources of progressive anti-government analysis are the monthlies: *Este País Mes a Mes* (published by CEASPA) and *Diálogo Social* (published by CSS). (See Appendix 3)

Radio

Radio is the most important communications media in Panama. Virtually all Panamanians have their one or two favorite radio stations among the some two dozen stations in the country. Unlike television, radio reaches even the most remote villages. Even in the cities, many Panamanians prefer radio to television. Especially popular are the lively morning talk shows broadcast by most stations.

Some dozen radio stations were tied to the Noriega government. Radio Nacional, which broadcast throughout the entire country, was directly owned by the government and was bombed off the air some 70 hours after the U.S. invasion began. Other stations were owned by politicians associated with the government, including Radio Uno Soberana ("Toti" Suárez of PPR), Radio Musical (Nestor de Icaza of PRD), Radio Tevedos (FDP), Onda Popular (Ramón Sierio of PALA), Radio Ritmo (José Blandón, ex-PRD leader and Rubén Darío Murgas of PRD), Radio Tic Tac (Rigoberto Paredes of PRD), and Radio Cadena Millonaria (Balbino Macia of PRD). Three stations were owned by government or military officials: Radio Verbo (Manuel Noriega), Radio

Monumental (Manuel Solís Palma, president), and Radio América (Rodolfo Chiari De León, minister of Government and Justice).

At least four radio stations were closed down by the military government, including KW Continente (Rodrigo Correa, MOLIRENA), Radio Mundial and Radio Diez (Carlos Zuñiga, PAPO), and La Exitosa (Aristides de Icaza, also owner of Radio Alegre).

The country's most powerful radio network is Circuit RPC. Panama has two church-owned radio stations: Radio Hogar (Catholic) and La Voz del Istmo (Protestant). The U.S. Southern Command Network (SCN) operates AM and FM stations for the U.S. forces. Although primarily intended for U.S. military personnel and their families, these English-language stations also have a significant Panamanian audience.

Television

Television, the most conservative communications media in Panama, is influential, especially in the Panama City area where an estimated 75 percent of homes have television sets.[40] Television fare has been limited by the political views of its oligarchic and government owners. The stations often ban certain movies and creative programming that deals with social issues, calling them "subversive" or "pro-communist."

The country's Spanish-language TV stations carry similar programs (a mix of imported series including soap operas from Mexico and Venezuela). The oldest station, TV4 (Corporación Panameña de Radiodifusión) owned by members of the Eleta Almarán family, was initially a strong supporter of the Torrijos regime and is virulently anticommunist. TV2 (Televisora Nacional), formed in 1963, was owned by the Chiari family (including Minister of Government and Justice Rodolfo Chiari) but was sold in the late 1980s to individuals close to the PDF as part of a juicy business/political deal.[11] TV13 (Telemetro) has been mainly a movie channel and was owned by a group of PRD members who were active in the PRD businessmen's front. Channel 11, the educational station, is operated by the University of Panama and owned by the Ministries of Planning and Education. TV5 (Telecinco) was owned by the Delvalle family but has been purchased by other owners.

You can tune into English-language programming on SCN TV (Channels 8 and 10), which attract a significant Panamanian audience, or on cable TV. Visión Satelite (VISAT), established in 1987, provides cable programming.

Government Censorship and Control

Besides directly controlling a broad array of print and electronic media, the military regime restricted press freedom through a licensing system in which the Ministry of Government and Justice issued licenses for all working journalists, photographers, reporters, and editors. Only columnists were exempt from this licensing requirement. There were several cases of opposition journalists being denied licenses.

Much more serious than licensing was a 1978 law that allowed the government to enforce administrative sanctions, without any guarantees of due process, against any media outlet disseminating news the Ministry of Government and Justice considered false, insulting, or slanderous. This tight control of the press created a environment of self-censorship on the part of the media.

Roberto Eisenmann and *La Prensa* were repeated victims of government press restrictions in the 1980s. Eisenmann, the owner of banks in Miami as well as a conglomerate of department stores, banks, and real estate companies in Panama, was first exiled from Panama in 1976 by Torrijos. When he returned to the country in 1980, he founded *La Prensa*, which has been repeatedly shut down, reopened, and raided by the government. The paper, which enjoys a circulation of 50,000, was last closed in February 1988.[42]

The government crackdown on press freedom escalated in 1987 when, in response to mounting anti-government protests, it declared a state of emergency suspending all press freedoms and creating a board of censors to monitor the opposition press, which has since been all but eliminated. Foreign journalists also fell victim to increasing government attempts to curb the media. Numerous foreign journalists, including Sam Dillon of the *Miami Herald*, were run out of the country. Others were turned back at the airport.

U.S. Government Information Services

As in other countries, the U.S. government disseminates written and electronic news through USIS, the overseas branch of the U.S. Information Agency (USIA). In Panama, the U.S. government also coordinated clandestine broadcasting operations to prop up the Civic Crusade. The program began in 1988 with a secret FM station named Radio Constitucional, which soon went off the air.

Early in 1989 President Bush approved a $10 million covert operations plan for Panama that included clandestine broadcasting. These secret media operations were brought to a close this time by the Panamanian government in April 1989 when it arrested a U.S. businessman in charge of the clandestine broadcasting network and confiscated about $350,000 worth of radio and communications equipment from eight apartments around Panama City. The government charged that Washington was waging an "electronic war" as part of its destabilization campaign. The secret radio operation, however, represented no real threat since few Panamanians outside the government knew or cared about the clandestine station.[43]

Access to U.S. news is not a problem in Panama because viewers can easily tune into the U.S. Southern Command's radio and television stations, where in addition to getting a full complement of U.S.-style reporting one is treated to frequent renditions of patriotic music, including "God Bless America." A 1988 report in the *Columbia Journalism Review* concluded that U.S. journalists follow the lead of the White House in their reporting. The article by Ken Silverstein noted that the U.S. press was largely silent about the fraudulent 1984 elections, paralleling the U.S. government's own "see-no-evil approach" at the time. "Recently—and only recently—coverage has focused on General Manuel Antonio Noriega, who has been portrayed as a thug presiding over a corrupt regime. Any reporter with even a minimum of initiative—or encouragement of an alert editor—could have written this story years ago."[44]

The State of Health

Health conditions in Panama compare favorably to most other Central American countries, with the exception of Costa Rica and Belize. As elsewhere in the region, Panama saw a steady improvement in health care in the 1970s that resulted in improving mortality rates and increased life expectancy.

The life expectancy at birth is 73 years (1986), compared to 61 years in Guatemala and 75 years in the United States. Infant mortality (during the first year) dropped from 105 per thousand births in 1960 to 23 per thousand in 1986.[45]

These sanguine statistics are somewhat shadowed by the widening gap between rural and urban health conditions. The areas of the country of least population density (Darién, Bocas del Toro, Veraguas, Los Santos, Colón) are the areas with the lowest levels of health care and the lowest per capita income. The difference between rural and urban areas is sometimes extreme, as in the case of the largely Indian town of Tolé in Chiriquí where the life expectancy in 1976 was only 38 years.[46] In remote rural areas the causes of death are largely preventable and transmittable illnesses related to poor diet, lack of access to medical care, and contaminated water supplies. In urban areas and more accessible rural areas, however, the most prevalent causes of death are cancer, accidents and other violent deaths, and heart failure, paralleling patterns found in the industrial world.[47] In mid-1989 the Ministry of Health reported that Panama is among the countries most affected by AIDS. During the first six months of 1989, 86 AIDS-related deaths were reported.[48]

There is a marked correlation between location and population rate. Urban women have an average of 2.7 children, rural women have more than five children.[49] Contraception devices are widely available, especially in urban areas. Some 70 percent of married women who want to avoid having children have used contraceptives — compared to 45 percent in Guatemala.

A 1982 study by the Ministry of Health found that more than 20 percent of families suffered from inadequate nutrition and that 10 percent of children under five suffered from severe malnutrition. Some 30 percent of school-age children showed signs of slow development, most likely related to malnutrition.[50]

The U.S. government and military have exercised a beneficial influence on the state of health in Panama. From the beginning of the U.S. impact on Panamanian internal affairs, health has always been an important issue. In constructing the canal, yellow fever and malaria were the main obstacles. To maintain favorable conditions for Canal Zone residents and U.S. military personnel, the United States has encouraged the Panamanian government to improve its public health system, and during the construction period put in running water, sewage facilities, and paved roads in Panama City and Colón.

A U.S.-financed study of health care in Panama by Dr. Ira Falk made a series of recommendations about steps needed to improve the public-sector health care system. Many of the 59 recommendations made by Falk were eventually adopted by the government in the early 1960s. In 1963 the government published its first National Health Plan in conjunction with Alliance for Progress projects.

The 1968 coup by the National Guard signaled the beginning of a renewed and expanded government commitment to improving the country's health care. The Torrijos regime launched a national campaign which included the formation of community "Health Committees" throughout the country. The government created a new Ministry of Health to coordinate and assist the grassroots work of the Health Committees, which sponsored latrine, water, popular education, and communal vegetable projects. The health committees also developed productive economic projects designed to cover the costs of new health centers. The number of doctors doubled between 1970 and 1979 and the number of health care facilities jumped 70 percent.[51] In 1988 there were 6.9 physicians per 10,000 inhabitants.[52]

The country's social security system also expanded rapidly in the 1970s, but is now in serious financial difficulties. Although the general population doubled during the decade, those covered by social security tripled, incorporating many aging workers into the system. Workers of the United Fruit Company were brought into the system, thereby relieving the company of its former responsibility of providing health care benefits to its employees. Many of these workers are now retiring and represent a severe strain on the system. But the most serious problems facing social security have been the government's practice of dipping into its coffers to cover other government expenses and its own failure to contribute its obligated share to the system. Corruption and the absence of a profitable investment policy have also weakened this important source of health care.[53] The country's social security system is likely be one of the first targets of post-invasion austerity and structural-adjustment programs.

Religion

Since the Spanish Conquest the Roman Catholic church has been the dominant religious organization in Panama. The country became the seat of the first diocese established in the Western Hemisphere, and its colonial churches are constant reminders of the wealth and power of the early Catholic church in Panama. The cathedral in Panamá Viejo, which was ransacked and burned in 1671 by Welsh pirate Henry Morgan, remains the centerpiece of Panamá Viejo—a major tourist attraction.

Currently there is one archdiocese which includes the provinces of Panamá and Coclé. The balance of the country is divided into three dioceses of David (Chiriquí), Chitre (Herrera and Los Santos), and Santiago (Veraguas), and the special jurisdictions of Colón, San Blas, and Bocas del Toro. Since 1969 the leading figure in the church has been Archbishop Marcos McGrath, a Panamanian who before becoming archbishop presided over the Santiago diocese and was a theology professor at the Catholic University of Chile.

Catholicism is taught in public schools, but the instruction in not obligatory. In 1981 it was estimated that 86 percent of the population identified themselves as Catholic while 12 percent were Protestant/evangelical.[54] (In Panama, as elsewhere in Latin America, the term *evangélico* is frequently used to refer to all non-Catholic Christians.)

Despite its dominant position, the Catholic church in Panama is a weak institution. Less than 20 percent of the country's self-identified Catholics regularly attend mass. This lack of a strong social base is reflected in the small number of local vocations. At least 75 percent of Catholic clergy are foreign missionaries.[55] In 1980 there was only one priest to serve 6300 Catholics.[56] Strong participation by the laity through such organizations as the Delegates of the Word partially compensates for the low number of clergy.

In the mid-1970s the U.S. bishops funded a study to determine how the Panamanian church could become more self-sufficient. One result of that study were annual fundraising campaigns that by 1986 were providing the church with $800,000 in annual income. Contributions by church members began to fall dramatically in 1987, seriously endangering the institutional stability of the church. Lack of funds have also undermined its ambitious evangelizing campaign at a time when pentecostal churches have increased their own evangelization.[57]

Politics and the Church

Before the 1960s the Catholic church had little social or political presence in Panama. Its clergy dedicated themselves almost exclusively to administering the sacraments, celebrating mass, and operating schools. Involvement in education, including a Catholic university, was regarded as an effective way to maintain and extend the influence of the church, particularly among the society's ruling class. Overall, the church by its passive social role served to legitimize oligarchic control in Panama.[58]

In the 1950s the church hierarchy did form the Federation of Christian Leagues to counteract leftist influence among peasant communities. But it was not until after Vatican II that the church actively began defending and promoting the interests of the country's poor majority. This identification with the poor deepened after the Medellín Bishops' Conference in 1968, which advocated that the church assume a "preferential option for the poor." As part of the renovation process spurred by Vatican II and Medellín, the church placed more emphasis on the participation of the laity. As part of that effort the church hierarchy promoted the slogan "Christian, you are the church."[59]

The church founded peasant training and popular education organizations such as the Center for Social Instruction (CCS) and the Center for Research, Promotion, and Social Assistance (CEPAS). Through the John XXIII Center, the church formed and trained community cooperatives.[60] A center for this new social role was in the Veraguas region, presided over by Bishop McGrath until 1968. McGrath spearheaded an economic development plan for the area called Plan Veraguas, which received government backing and was implemented in close cooperation with U.S. Alliance for Progress and Peace Corps projects.

This developmentalist orientation of the institutional church later paralleled and legitimized the populist politics of the Torrijos regime. The church's commitment to social causes was reaffirmed in 1969 with the appointment of Marcos McGrath to head the Archdiocese of Panama. For the first time the church began to speak out on social issues, denouncing injustices and circulating pastoral letters on such issues as the 1977 Canal Treaties and the controversial Cerro Colorado copper mine.

Encouraged by the church hierarchy, many poor urban and rural communities formed Christian Base Communities (CBCs) throughout the country. These CBCs, most of which adopted the precepts of the theology of liberation, soon formed a left flank within the church which was self-described as the Popular Church. Although rhetorically committed to "the preferential option for the poor," the institutional church led by McGrath took an increasingly defensive posture in the face of the growing independence and militancy of the CBCs. This discrepancy between rhetoric and activism led to the increased isolation of the CBCs within the institutional church, although elements within the church hierarchy remained fully committed to practicing "the preferential option for the poor."

Symptomatic of the move of the institutional church away from progressive reforms was its alliance with the oligarchy to oppose the educational reform proposed by the Torrijos government in the late 1970s. The church together with the APEDE businessmen's group opposed the measure because they felt that the introduction of social issues into the curriculum would facilitate the spread of communism.[61]

Several factors contributed to the radicalization of the CBCs and other socially committed elements of the church. One was the influence of an activist and politically progressive sector of the foreign clergy. Another was the failure of the developmentalism and populism of the church and government to resolve the structural causes of poverty. Yet another radicalizing factor was the development of a strong Central American solidarity movement within the church. The examples of Nicaraguan, Guatemalan, and Salvadoran church activists inspired Panamanian Catholics. In the early 1980s the assassination of Archbishop Romero of El Salvador was commemorated by large processions through downtown Panama City. A local martyr revered by the Panamanian church activists is Reverend Héctor Gallego, who was kidnapped and assassinated in 1971, presumably for his strong commitment to the struggles of the poor in his parish in Veraguas.[62]

In 1983 the political right organized a campaign of defamation about the sectors of the church associated with liberation theology. A nationally publicized attempt by the right wing to discredit the CBCs in Chiriquí was directed against the Vicentian, Augustinian, and Jesuit priests working with the poor communities of the area. It was claimed in a letter to the bishop that the priests excluded people of other social classes, abused the liturgy, and constituted a national security threat because they backed the Nicaraguan Sandinistas. Shortly following this incident the Committee to Defend Democracy in Nicaragua, Panama, and Central America formed to continue the attacks against the socially committed church. Heading the Committee was Dulcidio González, president of the National Council of Private Business and chief of the Liberal Party.[63] The Panamanian Bishops' Conference vigorously defended the priests under attack.

The popular church, while not as strong as it was in the late 1970s, remains an influential sector within the Catholic church. CBCs are especially active in Chiriquí, Darién, and San Miguelito near Panama City. Some Protestant churches, especially the Lutheran and Methodist churches, also support the CBCs. A robust countervailing trend within the Catholic church that has the support of the archbishop is the spiritualist Charismatic movement which has more in common with the emotion-charged Christianity of groups like the Full Gospel Businessmen's Association than with the socially committed popular church.

Although most of the Catholic clergy had from the beginning thrown their support to the Civic Crusade, it was not until after the May 1989 elections that the church hierarchy aligned itself openly with the opposition. Church organizations had received U.S. funds to monitor the elections (See Nongovernmental Organizations), and circulated a pastoral letter condemning the election fraud. Archbishop McGrath even invited the Civic Crusade leaders to stand by him while he delivered his May 29, 1988 sermon accusing the Noriega regime of being illegitimate and repressive. In response, the government-linked Radio Nacional called for the expulsion of all foreign priests.

Protestantism to Pentecostalism

Protestant missionaries have been active in the territory that is now Panama since the early 1800s. In 1815 a mulatto Methodist preacher,

Mother Abel, accompanied a group of Jamaican and English immigrants who settled at Careening Bay in western Panama. Her mission was later passed to the the Wesleyan Methodists.[64] The Christ Church By-the-Sea, established by the Protestant Episcopal church in 1864 in Colón, was the second non-Catholic church built in Central America, the oldest being St. John's Cathedral founded in 1825 in Belize City.

The construction of the Panama Canal marked the beginning of era of Protestant evangelism. Originally limited to the West Indians and U.S. citizens working on the canal, Protestant missionaries later extended their mission to the country's *mestizo* population. Today more than two-thirds of the country's Protestants are Spanish-speaking. Although missionaries have been evangelizing among the Indian community, especially the Kuna, since the early 1900s, it was not until the 1950s that serious outreach work began. Among the most active groups has been the New Tribes Mission, which has had as many as 60 U.S. missionaries working among Panama's indigenous communities.

Historically the largest Protestant churches in Panama have been the Church of the Foursquare Gospel and the Seventh Day Adventists. Beginning its missionary work in 1928, by 1960 the Church of the Foursquare Gospel had become the country's largest Protestant denomination, a position that it held at least until the late 1970s. The more traditional Protestant denominations (including Wesleyan Methodist, Southern Baptist Convention, Episcopal, Lutheran, and Church of Christ) have been largely eclipsed by the Pentecostal churches. Leading the way was the Foursquare Church, but since the early 1970s it has been newer Pentecostal churches like Assemblies of God and Church of God that have been the most dynamic forces in the evangelical movement.

Between 1960 and 1978 the overall rate of growth of Protestantism was 4.7 percent. Most of this growth has taken place among the *mestizo* population, and virtually all the increase has been among the new U.S. Pentecostal churches that began establishing missions in the 1960s. While the upper classes have largely retained their cultural and religious identification with the Catholic church, such transnational organizations as the Full Gospel Businessmen's Association and Women's Aglow Fellowship have made important inroads into middle- and upper-class Catholic communities.

The first U.S.-sponsored evangelical crusade was that of T. L. Osborn in the early 1950s among the West Indian population of Colón. Although currently active in Panama, the Latin American Mission did not bring its Costa Rica-based Evangelism In-Depth crusade to Panama. The healing campaigns of the Assemblies of God have found great resonance in

Panama. Evangelical crusades have also been sponsored by the Alfa y Omega (Campus Crusade for Christ).

The political and economic crisis of the late 1980s proved a great boon to the evangelical churches, which preach a moral and political conservatism. Although still a minority, the Protestant/evangelical community is expanding fast, challenging the traditional religious and cultural hold of the Catholic church.

Nongovernmental Organizations

Church service organizations from the United States have been in Panama since the early 1900s. The Episcopal church of the United States has, for example, had religious and charitable operations in Panama since 1907. In the 1940s and 1950s U.S. missionary organizations, both Catholic and evangelical, began placing staff in the country. Among the earliest were the Maryknoll Sisters, Mennonite Brethren Mission, and Gospel Missionary Union.

The first U.S. private, nongovernmental organization (NGO) that established operations in Panama was CARE, an NGO created to distribute U.S. food aid, which has been active in the country since 1953. It was not until the 1960s that foreign NGOs, mainly from the United States, became common in Panama. This new influx of private charitable and development organizations was sparked by the Alliance for Progress program and the creation of the U.S. Agency for International Development (AID). Among those AID-linked NGOs that entered Panama in the 1960s were Catholic Relief Services (CRS), Partners of the Americas, American Institute for Free Labor Development (AIFLD), and the Pan American Development Foundation (PADF). By the early 1980s there were over 50 U.S. NGOs and church organizations operating in Panama.

Until late 1987 when AID closed its offices in Panama, many U.S. and Panamanian NGOs received funding directly from the local AID Mission. Funding of several local NGOs continued through the U.S. embassy's Office of Development Affairs. These include the Panamanian White Cross (CBP), Private Sector Council for Educational Assistance (COSPAE), and the National Charity for Rural Panamanian Youth (PANAJURU).[65]

The closing of the AID Mission did not shut off the flow of AID funding for U.S. NGOs. Organizations like AIFLD (See Labor), PADF, and International Executive Service Corps have received funding for their Panama operations directly from the AID's Washington office. Another U.S. source of funding for local NGOs is the National Endowment for

Democracy (NED), a quasi-private foundation established with funds from the U.S. Information Agency (USIA) and AID. It is expected that AID in 1990 will renew and probably increase support for NGOs through a variety of its funding channels.

In 1984 NED funds to AIFLD in Panama were directed to presidential campaign of the government's candidate, Nicolás Ardito Barletta, through the AIFLD-sponsored Confederation of Workers (CTRP).[66] NED also financed business promotion and civic-awareness projects closely connected with the anti-Noriega opposition. NED supported business promotion programs, high school courses to promote free enterprise values, political training, and human rights monitoring by Panamanian Business Executive Association (APEDE) and the Center for Administrative Studies (CESA). APEDE was a member of the opposition Civic Crusade.[67] NED funds also supported political-education and civic-awareness programs of the Youth Civic Development Program of the local branch of the YMCA.[68]

Through the international institutes of the U.S. Republican Party (NRI) and the U.S. Democratic Party (NDI), NED played a major role in May 1989 elections. The two institutes provided election-monitoring training to organizations associated with the Civic Crusade, including the Catholic church. They also sponsored and organized a U.S. election-monitoring team. In addition, these NED groups were instrumental in building the Civic Crusade coalition by providing party-building and coalition training for the political opposition.[69] The AID-funded Center for Democracy, headed by Allen Weinstein, monitored the election in Panama. Immediately after the election, Weinstein authored an article in the *Wall Street Journal* in which he said the time had come to review the 1977 Canal Treaties and under what circumstances the United States should consider the use of force in Panama.[70]

The relief efforts following the U.S. invasion spurred a flurry of U.S. NGO activity in Panama. Among the main private organizations sending relief supplies were the American Red Cross, AmeriCares (through Knights of Malta), Catholic Relief Services, Direct Relief International, MAP International, Project Hope, and World Vision.[71]

Women and Feminism

Panama has a long and proud history of feminist activism. The Feminist National Party (PNF), founded in 1923, was one of the first feminist parties in Latin America. The party spearheaded the women's suffrage campaign in Panama, and through its Women's Cultural School pushed for social reforms benefiting women and children. In the 1930s the PNF protested the government's issuing of citizenship identity cards only to men. The party's antigovernment positions made its leaders and members targets for government reprisals. All the PNF-associated university professors were terminated in 1938. In 1944 many former PNF members founded the National Women's Union, which renewed the struggle for women's right to vote. The long suffrage fight finally bore fruit in a 1944 government decree allowing the female vote and another decree the next year establishing equal rights for women.[72]

The UN declaration in 1975 establishing the International Women's Year sparked a new era of feminist organizing and consciousness-raising. Having won the right to vote, Panamanian women had pushed aside the main legal impediment to their full participation in society and politics. But many other institutional and socio-cultural obstacles kept full equality for women an unrealized goal.

The government ratified the international convention calling for the elimination of all forms of discrimination against women. Yet sexist provisions of the country's Civil Code and Family Code have maintained women as second-class citizens. Widows and divorcees are prohibited from remarrying until 300 days after the death of the husband or a divorce decree—prohibitions that do not apply to men. Legal justifications for divorce include a one-time extramarital affair on the part of the wife and "scandalous concubinity" (a permanent extramarital affair) on the part of the husband. Upon contracting marriage, a woman is by law required to add the husband's last name to her own.[73]

Among the Central American countries Panama has the highest level of female participation in the workforce. Nevertheless, women workers suffer widespread discrimination. Not uncommonly women are required to take a pregnancy test; preferential employment goes to single women who are then laid off if they become pregnant. To avoid having to pay the government-mandated severance payment, employers often have women workers sign three-month contracts. Women constitute 57 percent of post-secondary school enrollment, but higher education levels do not necessarily mean equal pay. The International Labor Office (ILO) found that while median monthly income of both men and women increases significantly with increased education, the disparity between the monthly incomes of men and women increases rather than diminishes with the level of education.[74]

The economic crisis has hit poor women hard, forcing many mothers into the workforce. The female labor force is growing much faster than the male labor force, and the number of woman-headed households has also increased dramatically in the last decade. While 23 percent of higher-income women head households in the Panamanian urban sector, the percentage rises to 37 percent among lower-income women (compared to a corresponding 22 percent in neighboring Costa Rica) — one of the highest rates in Latin America.[75] Many lower-class women work as domestics, an occupation not protected by the Labor Code and as a result one with no specified free time or work-day length. Another common source of employment for working-class women is the export-oriented industrial sector. Laboring in sweatshop conditions, thousands of Panamanian women assemble clothes for export for such textile companies as Vanity Fair, Intimate, Gregor, and Durex.[76]

The two main sources of feminist thought are at the national university — at its Center for Women's Development (CEDEM) and University World Service Committee (SUM) — and at such research and popular education organizations as the Panamanian Social Study and Action Center (CEASPA) and Center for Social Instruction (CCS). In the past, the government and the Revolutionary Democratic Party (PRD) sponsored several women's organizations such as the Popular Feminist Front and the National Federation of Democratic Women. There also existed an anti-imperialist women's organization called the Women's Front Against Aggression (FUMCA). Numerous female professional associations, church groups, and wings of labor unions and political parties also exist.

While the feminist movement is largely leftist and anti-imperialistic, women played a major role in supporting the National Civic Crusade. In an analysis of this phenomenon, a 1987 article in the local *Diálogo Social* speculated that women were attracted to the anti-government, oligarchy-backed movement because of its tone of moral outrage. Politically inexperienced churchwomen and housewives provided an important activist base for this movement.[77]

Minorities and Native Peoples

Spanish-speaking *mestizos* account for about 70 percent of the population. Blacks compose the largest minority sector — divided between those of colonial/slave descent (about 8 percent) and those of West Indian origin (about 5 percent). A white *criollo* sector, about 10 percent of the population, dominates the society's economic elite. The Indian population, divided among several different tribes, accounts for about 4 percent of the Panamanian population.

The first blacks came to the country as slaves from Africa, and their descendants are found in dispersed pockets of black communities along the country's Atlantic coast and in small isolated villages in Darién. The second group of Panama's blacks came from the Caribbean islands under contracts to work on the railroad or the canal. Other Caribbean blacks immigrated to seek work on the banana plantations in Chiriquí and Bocas del Toro. Because of their origin, the term *antillanos* (Antilleans) has long been associated with the country's black population, which is concentrated in the urban corridor of Panama City and Colón and in Puerto Armuelles.[78]

Although the black community is more integrated socially than in other Central American countries (with the exception of Belize), blacks are still widely considered as second-class citizens. This treatment dates back to the early 1900s when during the construction of the Panama Canal white workers were paid in gold while the *antillanos* and many *mestizo* workers were compensated in silver.[79] White workers received as much as 4 times more than their black counterparts. In the Canal Zone, the housing, restaurants, hospitals, and other services all belonged to the U.S. government, and all practiced segregation.[80] In the 1950s the U.S. administrators of the canal pushed the blacks out of the Canal Zone to avoid civil rights protests, creating a type of apartheid.[81]

The U.S. government was not the only perpetrator of racism; the Panamanian oligarchy and middle class also encouraged racist sentiments and practices. The Harvard-educated Arnulfo Arias fomented racist sentiments in the Communal Action movement of the 1920s. Arias and others regarded the blacks as foreign competitors for the benefits of the Canal Zone. In the 1930s Arias organized a nationalist-populist coalition that launched him to the presidency in 1940. Although progressive in some respects, Arias was a confirmed racist and pushed through a new constitution that prohibited further immigration of blacks and denied them basic civil rights, such as the right to own property, unless they could demonstrate a familiarity with the Spanish language and Panamanian history.[82]

Antillanos have not generally shared the nationalist sentiments of the *mestizo* population, but they have integrated themselves into the country's labor and popular movements. They led strikes for higher wages and food, braved U.S. military repression of their union movement in 1920, and were active in the 1925 Renters' Movement.[83] Protests and organizing by black workers have gradually eliminated the most blatant forms of discrimination in the Canal Zone, although racism persists.

The advent of *torrijismo* in 1968 helped end the historical monopoly of power by white Panamanians. As a result of this new anti-oligarchic populism, blacks were more easily accepted into the government, security forces, and even business. Large numbers of blacks have become culturally Hispanicized and are now accepted as bona fide *panameños*. Throughout Panama blacks have fewer work opportunities than whites and *mestizos* – in part for lack of good connections but also because of underlying racism.

Native Panamanians

Five different indigenous groups exist in Panama. The Guaymí, the most numerous with 54,000 tribal members, live in western Panama in Bocas del Toro on the Atlantic side and in the provinces of Chiriquí and Veraguas on the Pacific side. The Kuna, with an estimated 30,000 members, live mainly on the San Blas islands off the country's northeastern coast but are also found in settlements along the Gulf of Urabá (bordering Colombia) and in the Darién province. The Chocó Indians, with an estimated 25,000 members, live in the Pacific lowlands of the Darién province. Small numbers of Teribe and Bokota Indians live in the western *cordillera*.

When the Spanish first explored the northwestern Caribbean coastline, they encountered several Indian tribes. Besides the Guaymí, Térrabas, Talamancas, Cabégaras, Changuena, and Dorasque Indians also inhabited this region. Raids by the Spanish decimated these Indian tribes, pushing them inland and into Costa Rica. Gold which area Indians acquired through trade with Colombian Indians was confiscated, and many Indians were kidnapped and sold as slaves.[84] In the 17th and 18th centuries the Guaymí were the target of raids by Nicaraguan Miskito Indians organized by British colonizers.[85] The remaining Guaymí society has been further disrupted by the spread of banana plantations, the construction of the Inter-American Highway through their land, and the appropriation of their communal lands by *mestizo* peasants and cattle-ranching oligarchs.

Over the past two decades the Guaymí have organized to protect their land and culture. Through the Guaymí General Congress they have demanded that the government establish an autonomous Guaymí *comarca* (reserve) – a demand that was quashed in 1984 when the executive branch suspended talks and passed the problem to the Legislative Assembly. The Guaymí continue to petition for the right to administer justice in their own language and based on their own laws. They have also asked for protection against the incursion of evangelical sects, which are further weakening their culture.[86]

The commercial exploitation of Guaymí land by non-Indians combined with the tribe's own slash-and-burn type agriculture have degraded the environment, causing severe erosion in many areas, particularly in Chiriquí and Veraguas.[87] This environmental crisis has become one more cause of Guaymí poverty and unemployment. To make a living, many Guaymí males leave their homes to join the country's migrant workforce. On the coffee and banana plantations, they are generally relegated to the most dangerous and lowest-paying jobs. They are specifically singled out to work with the most toxic chemicals. When burns, cancer, and poisoning render the Guaymí workers useless, they are laid off with little or no severance pay.[88]

The Chocó Indians consider themselves to be two distinct peoples — the Embera and Wounan. They are not natives of Panama but migrated to the eastern Pacific lowlands in the late 18th century from western Colombia where most are Wounan and live in the Chocó province. Famous for their poison-tipped blowgun darts, bands of these Amerindians were brought in from Colombia by the Spanish to break the resistance of the Kuna Indians who inhabited the Darién region.[89] Settlements previously inhabited by the Kuna were seized by these immigrant peoples, who later also moved into the areas abandoned by the Spanish.

In the 1960s the Chocó Indians gradually began to organize themselves into self-government communities and to demand government recognition of their land rights and access to government services. In 1983 the government recognized the Comarca Embera-Drua, a reserve of 300,000 hectares which overlaps with the area classified as the Darién Biosphere Reserve. This victory has been soured by the steady environmental degradation of the reserve. Much of the reserve, particularly the areas surrounding the recently established villages, are depleted of game animals and wild plants. Accustomed to a hunter-gatherer economy, the Chocó Indians have turned increasingly to cash crops. Aggravating the environmental crisis is the steady encroachment of lumber companies and agricultural colonists from the western provinces.[90]

The Kuna have been the most successful in preserving their land and culture. It is not clear if the Kuna people inhabited the Darién region at the time of the Spanish conquest or if they migrated to the region from Colombia. Descriptions by Spanish expeditions and pirates in the 17th century, however, establish their presence in the Darién province.[91]

In the mid-19th century the Kuna began relocating many of their communities on the San Blas islands. Strategic concerns and the abundance of pests and disease in the Pacific lowlands were probably among the reasons for this migration. Strong local hierarchies developed on the occupied islands, and an elaborately organized political infrastructure developed.[92] The local governments were eventually integrated into the Kuna General Congress, which meets twice annually and establishes the direction of Kuna national politics. Three national chiefs preside over the Congress and act as the Kuna spokespersons to the Panamanian government and society.[93]

The establishment of the Comarca of San Blas in 1938 resulted from a long history of Kuna efforts to protect their land and culture. The self-chosen isolation of the Kuna on the San Blas islands proved key to the preservation of their culture and the development of a self-directed economy. On occasion, the islanders violently repelled European traders who tried to come ashore. In the early 1900s the Kuna people repeatedly clashed with non-Kuna rubber traders and agricultural colonists who were encroaching on tribal land. The Kuna revolted in 1925 against government acculturation programs and attempted control by government police. The now-celebrated 1925 revolt was also the result of accumulated tensions between the Kuna people and Catholic missionaries and colonists.[94]

The successful revolt, in which the Kuna Indians received assistance from North American adventurer Richard Marsh, led to a 1930 treaty reaffirming the partial autonomy of the San Blas region. Eight years later, the Kuna territory gained official status as a *comarca*.[95] The success story of the Kuna continues into the present with the development of a stable economy (based largely on tourism, crafts, coconuts, fishing, and cash transfers from Kunas employed in urban areas) and the maintenance of a strong cultural foundation. In 1985 the Kuna were the first Indian people to establish an internationally recognized forest reserve. The Kuna Wildlife Project, covering 60,000 hectares of rainforest within the *comarca* along the Caribbean coast, is being carefully preserved. The Kuna have founded a learning center in the reserve where non-Kuna are instructed in appropriate rainforest management techniques and scientists carry out rainforest research.[96]

Overall, the Kuna have been exceptional among Central American Indians. Not only did they survive the Spanish Conquest, but they also seemed to have emerged stronger and better organized from the regional turmoil during the centuries that followed. Partially due to the relative inaccessibility of their territory, they have kept outside influence to a minimum, enabling them to protect and promote their culture and lifestyle. Kuna traditions, such as the renowned cloth art of the Kuna women (the *mola*), are strongly anchored within Kuna society and Kunas are proud of their ethnic traditions—an attitude increasingly rare among the exploited and alienated Central American Indians.

Refugees and the Internally Displaced

Unlike other Central American countries, Panama does not have a significant refugee population. There are only about 1400 official refugees under international protection. The UN High Commission on Refugees (UNHCR) reported in 1988 that it provides assistance to some 200 Nicaraguans, 750 Salvadorans, and a small number of Guatemalans.[97] Under a cooperative program between UNHCR and the government, Salvadoran refugees were resettled in a remote jungle setting along the Atlantic coast where they have cleared land and are attempting to establish a self-sufficient community.

At least 17,000 Panamanians were displaced by the U.S. invasion and ensuing conflict. Displaced families, mainly from the poor neighborhoods where the fighting was most intense, found temporary refuge in schools and churches. When the firing stopped most of the displaced moved in with families and friends, although several thousand were cared for by the U.S. military, the U.S. Agency for International Development (AID), and U.S. private relief organizations. The U.S. government promised to rebuild the El Chorrillo neighborhood located next to the Panamanian military high command, which the U.S. invasion force destroyed. To provide new housing for the displaced, Washington has allocated $42 million mostly for private-sector construction programs.

The Endara government in February 1990 announced a "voluntary repatriation" program to deport an estimated 25,000 people who illegally entered the country in the past five years. Apparently the Noriega regime had netted over $200 million in the sale of visas and passports to foreigners, many of them Cubans.

Ecology and Environmentalism

More of the original forest cover remains in Panama than in any other Central American country, with the exception of Belize. Located below the hurricane belt and bathed in heavy rains, Panama hosts an abundance of tropical flora and fauna. More than 800 species of birds are found in Panama—more than found in the entire area of the Western Hemisphere north of the Tropic of Cancer. The country is aflutter with aviary life, with three of the four major migration routes between North and South America converging on Panama.[98] With coral reefs paralleling Panama on both sides and the most extensive mangrove area in Central America, Panama also hosts abundant sea life.[99]

Like other Central American countries, however, Panama faces severe environmental problems. This ecological crisis is most evident in the area of the canal and a small strip of Pacific lowlands west of the canal—the areas where 90 percent of Panamanians live. Most of the sewage from the two urban centers, Panama City and Colón, is discharged directly into coastal waters or canals and ditches that flow through the cities. This crisis is becoming increasingly evident along the Inter-American Highway to Darién.

Long stretches of mangroves are being cut down to make room for new urban developments, shrimp farms, and resorts, causing immense losses for the commercially important seafood industry. Mangrove bark, useful in the tanning industry, is being exported to Costa Rica, where the harvesting of red mangrove bark is prohibited. Birds, especially brightly plumed macaws and yellow-crowned parrots, are also commercially shipped out of the country as part of the international trade in exotic house pets.[100]

Deforestation and National Parks

Panama's low population density, the concentration of its population near the canal, and its diversified economic base have all contributed to the country's relatively large area of remaining tropical forest. About 60 percent of the country remains under some sort of forest cover.[101] Only 9 percent of the land base is dedicated to intensive annual cropping, but large areas are reserved for extensive livestock grazing.

Deforestation, nonetheless, is a rising concern in Panama. Since 1983 the annual deforestation rate has been 2.3 percent. In the 1980s over 97,000 acres of forest were lost each year, while only 9,000 acres were replanted annually. Panamanian ecologist Stanley Heckadon Moreno warns that by the year 2000 Panama could be a "desert with jungle representing less than 10 percent of the country." He predicts that the last forest areas will be located in Indian zones where production systems do not present an immediate threat to the environment.[102]

Soil erosion is a rising concern in Panama—where 50 percent of the soils are poor quality and 75 percent of the land is hillside terrain. Largely because of this severe rate of deforestation, about 20 percent of Panama was categorized as being seriously eroded or degraded. Soil-erosion rates in some of the country's prime agricultural areas are thought to be among the highest in all Latin America. The most critical soil erosion is taking place in the volcanic highlands of the Chiriquí province, especially around the Barú volcano.[103] The waterways that flow from this watershed are now filled with silt, causing severe losses to affected agricultural areas in the lowlands below the volcano.

Reacting to the demands of environmentalists, the government in 1987 announced a five-year suspension of tree-felling. The law prohibits the cutting of any primary forest or secondary forest over five years old. The main culprits of deforestation have been the cattle ranchers, who have encouraged peasants, especially in the Darién region, to clear frontier lands allowing them later to move in to graze cattle.[104]

A major environmental concern for Panama and the United States alike is the effect of deforestation on the Canal Area. A 1986 report by the Panama Ministry of Planning found that urbanization, slash-and-burn agriculture, cattle ranching, and road construction had deforested 70 percent of the watershed that provides the 52 million gallons of fresh water required daily by the canal locks. It has been projected that erosion and siltation from deforestation may reduce the capacity of the lake reservoirs for the canal operations as much as 10 percent by the year 2000.[105]

To avert this calamity, two national parks — Soberanía and Chagres — were created in the canal watershed. Together they account for almost half the watershed of the canal or some 600 square miles. As a result, the rate of deforestation in the canal watershed has slowed from 1100 acres a year before 1976 to 540 acres a year between 1984 and 1987. Deforestation has also presented a threat to the country's hydroelectric system which generates some 80 percent of the country's electricity, in the Bayano area and in Chiriquí.

International and local forces have combined to reserve a high percentage (8.7 percent) of the Panamanian land area as environmentally protected territory. Most of this protected space is found within four large national parks. La Amistad covers the the largest highland forest in Central America, extending into Costa Rica. Chagres covers the entire watershed of the Alajuela Lake and provides 40 percent of the water for the canal and is a major source of drinking water. Soberanía is a highly regarded spot for tropical botanical studies as well as a favorite recreational site. The Darién national park encompasses a large stretch along the Darién border with Colombia and is the largest protected area in Central America and has been declared a World Patrimony by UNESCO.[106]

Environmentalists Organize

Panama counts on a strong environmental movement. The leading organization is the National Association for the Conservation of Nature (ANCON), which receives significant support from such U.S. organizations as the Nature Conservancy and the John D. and Catherine T. Mac-Arthur Foundation. Founded in 1985 by academic and business leaders, ANCON's proclaimed mission is "exclusively to protect and conserve the natural resources and the biological diversity of Panama for the benefit of all the present and future generations of Panamanians."

ANCON has played a major role in supporting the creation and maintenance of the national park system but has been sharply criticized within Panama as being a cover for large business interests interested in gaining control over new resources. According to its critics, investors associated with ANCON have gained control over areas of the national parks for intended mining and development of tourism projects. It has also been noted that the environmental organization allied itself with the Civic Crusade.[107]

Another activist group is the Student Association for the Conservation of the Environment (ACECAP), which successfully pressured the government to protect a couple of endangered coastal areas on the relatively pristine Atlantic coastal region, which is now being spoiled by increasing oil spills and development projects.[108]

A strong grassroots environmental movement is being led by the Kuna Indians. They are working to protect and control development on their autonomous region of 5700 square miles which includes hundreds of coral islands and one of the largest remaining tracts of primary forest in Central America. Under Kuna direction, the Project for the Study and Management of Wild Areas of the Kuna Yala (PEMASKY) is attempting to create a biosphere reserve to protect their lands against peasant colonization and cattle ranching along a new road that cuts through the Comarca of Kuna Yala. Some Panamanians oppose this project because it is perceived as an attempt to increase Kuna autonomy and to hoard national resources.

The principal government organizations that involve themselves in environmental concerns are the Panamanian Institute of Renewable Resources (INRENARE) and the National Environmental Commission (CONAMA). The political and economic crisis in the late 1980s has drastically reduced the government's commitment to environmental protection due to shrinking government revenues. A ten-year $50 million AID natural resource management project was suspended in 1987.

The economic and political crisis in the cities during the late 1980s increased pressure on natural resources as people returned to rural areas and claimed more forest areas as a way to solve, albeit temporarily, their subsistence needs. The breakdown of authority following the U.S. invasion in late 1989 resulted in increased entry into "protected areas," creating more intractable difficulties.

Chapter 5

Foreign Influence

U.S. Foreign Policy

The United States — despite the constant aggravation of Panamanian nationalism — has usually succeeded in getting what it wants from Panama. From President Theodore Roosevelt's boast, "I took the canal, and let the Congress debate" to presidential candidate Ronald Reagan's assertion in 1976 that the Canal Zone is "sovereign U.S. territory" and that it "is ours and and we intend to keep it," U.S. arrogance has distinguished U.S.-Panamanian relations.

The price of this arrogance has been a deep reserve of anti-U.S. sentiment — at times dormant but on occasion flaring up in violent protests and rhetoric. The long colonial-style relationship between Washington and Panama has also given rise to a history of collaborative and subservient behavior on the part of Panamanians. All three elements — U.S. arrogance and Panamanian nationalism and obsequiousness — were factors in the events leading up to the U.S. invasion. In all likelihood, they will continue to characterize U.S.-Panamanian interactions in the 1990s.

U.S.-Panama Relations 1848-1979

The tensions between U.S. expansionism and the dignity of the Panamanian people can be traced back to the late 1840s. The discovery of gold in California in 1848 sparked a rush of steamship travel from New York to Chagres and from Panama City to San Francisco. Originally travel was by dug-out canoe and horseback. To speed travel across the isthmus, a concession was granted to the U.S.-owned Panama Railroad Company to build a railroad between Colón and Panama City.

The completion of the railroad eight years later left thousands of local people suddenly out of work and living in shacks in Panama City. In 1856, when a U.S. soldier without paying took a piece of watermelon from a street vendor, the explosive social situation erupted into what quickly became known as the *Tajada de Sandía* (Watermelon Slice) Incident. At least a dozen U.S. citizens were killed in the ensuing riot. Washington demanded and eventually received over $400,000 in indemnification for the families of the dead Americans. Several months later, 160 Marines landed to protect the railroad and impose U.S. control. This marked the first of five U.S. military interventions into Panama between 1856 and 1865.[1]

The Spanish-American War of 1898 marked the birth of the United States as an imperial power. U.S. military leaders, concerned that their gunboats had to travel the long route around Cape Horn, lobbied for the construction of an interoceanic canal across Panama. The Senate of Colombia rejected a U.S. petition in 1903 to build a canal through Panama, but their vote did not stop the United States or President Roosevelt. The U.S.S. Dixie and the U.S.S. Nashville sailed to Panama to prevent Colombia from squashing a U.S.-instigated revolt. A major figure in these machinations was William Nelson Cromwell, founder of the prestigious New York law firm Sullivan & Cromwell. Cromwell represented and owned stock in the French Canal Company and was a director of the Panama Railroad Company.

Only five days after securing Panama's independence from Colombia, the first canal treaty was signed with the United States. Signing the treaty for Panama was Frenchman Philippe Bunau-Varilla, who, like Cromwell, was interested in selling the remaining assets of the French company that had earlier tried to build a canal.

The treaty gave the United States the right to intervene in the internal affairs of the new country, which became an unofficial protectorate of the United States. U.S. government and military leaders supervised Panama's national elections in 1908, 1912, and 1918. Unlike other sectors of the population, the Panamanian oligarchy supported the U.S. presence in Panama and often requested the intervention of U.S. forces to control popular protests and uprisings. In 1918, a detachment of Marines arrived in the province of Chiriquí and stayed for two years to maintain public order. In 1925, 600 U.S. Army troops marched into Panama City to break a rent strike. For twelve days, American troops patrolled the streets to keep order and guard U.S. property.[2]

Popular opposition forced the Panamanian government to reject a largely concessionary treaty with the United States in 1926. It was not until the General Treaty of Friendship and Cooperation in 1936 that the United States relinquished the right to unilateral intervention in Panama's political affairs. In that treaty, the United States obtained access to additional lands and waters for the defense and modernization of the canal. In 1942 the U.S.-Panama Base Convention allowed the United States over one hundred new military and telecommunications facilities in Panama, beginning the extensive and permanent U.S. military presence in the Canal Zone. In 1947 popular protests prevented the authorization of increased U.S. military presence, but the Treaty of Mutual Understanding and Cooperation of 1955 permitted the United States to locate another large military base in Panama in exchange for increased commercial access to the Canal Zone by the local elite.[3]

Pent-up resentment against the United States surfaced in the Flag Riots of 1964 when disturbances broke out after Canal Zone residents prevented Panamanian high school students from raising the Panamanian flag alongside the U.S. flag in the Zone. "Within hours, 30,000 Panamanians were in the streets of Panama City, confronting U.S. troops who had orders to fire warning shots before shooting to kill. The riot soon spread to Colón, on the Atlantic side of the Zone, then deep into the interior....By the time this explosion of anti-Yankee fury was contained, over $2 million in property had been burned or otherwise destroyed — almost all of it American. Twenty-eight people had been killed, 300 wounded, and 500 arrested, almost all of them Panamanian."[4]

When the government of Panama reacted by breaking relations with Washington, the United States agreed to raise the Panamanian flag at the Canal Zone high school and to negotiate a new canal treaty that was soundly rejected by Panamanians. Finally in 1977, under the leadership of Omar Torrijos Herrera, Panama and the United States reached an agreement over the ownership and operation of the Panama Canal.[5]

Torrijos said: "Mr. President [Carter]...I want you to know that this treaty, which I shall sign and which repeals a treaty not signed by any Panamanian, does not enjoy the approval of all our people, because the 23 years agreed upon as a transition period are 8395 days, because during this time there will still be military bases which may make our country a strategic reprisal target, and because we are agreeing to a treaty of neutrality which places us under the protective umbrella of the Pentagon. This pact could, if it is not administered judiciously by future generations, become an instrument of permanent intervention."[6]

Since the first treaty in 1903 the United States had resisted attempts by Panamanians to obtain more control over the canal and the Canal Zone. In the 1960s, however, U.S. military analysts reported that they no longer considered the canal of strategic military importance since at least 24 of the largest U.S. aircraft carriers could not fit through the canal.[7] Military experts also noted that the most likely threat to the operation of the canal would come from within Panama by insurgents frustrated with continued U.S. domination of the canal and the Canal Zone. The military generally agreed that the best defense of the canal would be a cooperative, protective contract involving Panama's National Guard (later called the Panama Defense Forces).

On October 1, 1979 the Panama Canal Treaties signed in 1977 took effect. The first one, called simply the Panama Canal Treaty, governs the operation and defense of the canal by the United States through December 31, 1999. The second, Treaty on the Permanent Neutrality and Operation of the Panama Canal, guarantees the neutrality of the canal in peace and war. Among the provisions of two treaties are the following:

* Right of the United States to manage and operate the canal until the year 2000.

* The United States retained primary responsibility for the canal's defense during the Panama Canal Treaty's term with increasing participation by the Panama Defense Forces.

* Although the primary responsibility to defend the canal would end in the year 2000, the United States retained perpetual authority to protect and defend the canal in the event that the neutrality of the canal was threatened.

* All key bases and training areas operated by the United States to remain under U.S. control until the year 2000.

* Appropriation of territorial jurisdiction by Panama in 1979 over the Canal Zone (five-mile area on either side of the canal).

* Establishment of a nine-member board, composed of five U.S. members and four Panamanian members, to manage the newly created Panama Canal Commission.

"The United States basically won on the treaties," commented Mario Galindo, a lawyer in Panama who led the local opposition to their ratification. "In fact, the new treaties make us more subservient to the Americans than ever. The 1903 treaties at least pretended Panama was sovereign. The 1977 treaties give the United States the right to intervene here without even asking permission."[8] The Neutrality Treaty has no termination date. Under its provisions, the United States and Panama both guarantee the neutrality of the canal "in order that both in time of peace and in time of war it shall remain secure and open to peaceful transit by the vessels of all nations on terms of entire equality."

Post-Treaty Relations: Calm After the Storm

Washington's relations with Panama significantly improved after the Canal Treaties went into effect in 1979. The flames of Panamanian nationalism were extinguished as the fences that enclosed the Canal Zone were torn down. Contrary to the predictions of the U.S. rightists who had opposed the treaties, canal revenues increased in the 1980s and the country's National Guard showed great interest in its new role as the joint defender of the canal. With the tensions around the control of the canal resolved for the moment, U.S. and other foreign investors found Panama a more stable place to do business. The American Chamber of Commerce in Panama formed in 1979, and the country's international servicing operations, particularly the offshore banking center and the Colón Free Zone, prospered.

Instead of pulling further away from U.S. hegemony, Panama, as a result of the treaties, drew closer to U.S. foreign policy. After 1979, the U.S. Southern Command (SOUTHCOM), headquartered in the Canal Zone (now called the Canal Area), expanded its operations — contrary to all the predictions of the U.S. anti-treaty forces.[9] Beginning in 1979, joint military maneuvers between U.S. forces and the National Guard deepened the relationship between the two armed forces. Broadly interpreting the treaty provision for defense of the canal, these maneuvers extended as far as the Costa Rican border.

The improved relations with Panama resulting from the treaties proved providential for the aggressive foreign policy of President Reagan. SOUTHCOM, which had been one of the Pentagon's sleepiest military commands, suddenly started to buzz with activity. Some contras were trained at U.S. bases, and aerial surveillance missions over Nicaragua and El Salvador took off daily from the SOUTHCOM's air bases.

Under Torrijos, the National Guard and the Panamanian government had charted out an independent foreign policy. But with Torrijos' death in 1981, Panama once again started to fall in line with U.S. foreign policy. The new National Guard commander, Gen. Rubén Darío Paredes, was by 1983 aligning himself with the U.S. anti-Sandinista counterrevolution. The Panamanian Defense Forces (PDF), under Gen. Manuel Antonio Noriega, continued this shift away from the nonaligned foreign policy adopted by Torrijos. Panama even reactivated its observer status with the revived regional military alliance CONDECA, which was pushed forward by SOUTHCOM Commander Gen. Paul Gorman as a way to further isolate Nicaragua.[10] At one point, Noriega offered to assist operations to assassinate the Sandinista leadership. This collaboration with U.S. military strategy in the region put the PDF at odds with the Foreign Ministry's promotion of the peace process through Contadora, pointing to the growing contradictions between the PDF's profession of nationalism and populism and its uncritical cooperation with SOUTHCOM.[11]

An Old Affair Turns Bitter

The U.S. partnership with Noriega dated back to late 1959 when Noriega, then a student at a military academy in Peru, began supplying U.S. officials information about the leftist sympathies of fellow students.[12] This relationship did not become contractual until 1967 when, as intelligence officer under Major Omar Torrijos, Captain Noriega regularly supplied intelligence information to the CIA.[13] In 1967 Noriega also signed up for intelligence and counter-intelligence training at Fort Gulick and went to Fort Bragg, North Carolina for a course in psychological operations (PSYOPS), where he learned the art of media manipulation to conquer adversaries and control internal enemies.[14]

In 1970 Noriega became the Chief of Intelligence for the Torrijos regime which had seized power two years before. He used his new position to expand his intelligence work, hiring himself out to the Cubans, Israelis, and Taiwanese. Although aware of Noriega's double-dealing, the CIA insisted that his allegiance was first to the United States. The State Department called him the "rent-a-colonel."

The U.S. government was also aware, perhaps as early as the late 1960s, that Noriega and the National Guard were raking in bribes, payoffs, and commissions from the drug trade. In 1972, during the Nixon administration, one Drug Enforcement Agency (DEA) official even suggested that Noriega be assassinated.[15] The DEA turned down the plan but did warn Torrijos that it was aware of Noriega and the National Guard's connections to drug traffickers. By the beginning of the Carter administration the liabilities of dealing with Noriega were judged too great and his contract with U.S. intelligence agencies was withdrawn. The case against Noriega intensified in the late 1970s when U.S. intelligence found that Noriega was associated with Panamanians running guns to the Sandinista rebels in Nicaragua. In January 1980, however, the CIA pressured U.S. prosecutors to drop their plans to indict the Panamanian gun runners because the Torrijos regime had granted the Shah of Iran asylum in Panama as a favor to the United States.

After Noriega maneuvered his way to the head of the PDF in 1983, the Reagan administration renewed his contracts with the CIA and Defense Intelligence Agency, which amounted to nearly $200,000 annually. Washington was not unaware that Noriega and the PDF were in league with the Medellín drug cartel but judged the PDF collaboration in U.S.

foreign policy objectives, especially the contra war, a more important concern. Contras were trained in Panama, and in the spring of 1985 Noriega helped arrange a sabotage attack on a Nicaraguan arsenal. In 1984 Noriega also provided at least $100,000 to a contra leader, according to a document released for Oliver North's trial. Any help for the contra cause blinded the Reagan administration to Noriega's transgressions, observed Senator Patrick Leahy who then served on the Senate Intelligence Committee.[16]

No one factor, however, can explain the U.S. campaign of destabilization against the Noriega regime. In the mid-1980s U.S. foreign policy in Panama seemed to be caught between two forces. On the one side were the pragmatists in the CIA, Department of Defense, and the Reagan administration who put a premium on political stability in Panama at a time when U.S. attention was focused on Nicaragua and El Salvador. Noriega, for all his faults, was seen as a reliable ally. On what turned out to be the winning side of this debate were the rightwing and neoconservative ideologues who had lost the battle against the canal treaties and regarded the PDF-controlled government as a less than reliable ally in the battle against leftist advances in Central America.[17]

In 1986 relations between Washington and Panama's strongman grew increasingly testy. Elliott Abrams and Senator Jesse Helms teamed up in attacking Noriega in congressional hearings, and the National Security Council (NSC) determined that Noriega was becoming less than fully cooperative in U.S. efforts to topple the Sandinistas. The propaganda war against Noriega was unleashed in June 1986 when *New York Times* reporter Seymour Hersh published a series of articles about Noriega which badly embarrassed the administration.

The final links of cooperation between Noriega and Washington were broken in 1987 as a result of the Iran-Contra revelations and the crumbling of U.S. hopes for the military counterrevolution against Nicaragua. The death of CIA chief William Casey, a Noriega advocate, further isolated Noriega.

Washington set out to demonize Noriega, blaming him for the drug problem in the United States and for most of Panama's internal problems. As Richard Millet noted in a *Foreign Policy* essay in mid-1988, U.S. foreign policy labeled Noriega as "the cause rather than the product of most of Panama's problems." Furthermore, "The real issues are the basic weaknesses in Panama's political, social, and economic structures— weaknesses that stem from the internal and external forces that have shaped the country's recent past." Paramount among these forces has been "the massive influence of America and the U.S.-controlled canal."[18]

Destabilization and Invasion

To rid the country of Noriega, U.S. economic and military aid was cut off, the propaganda war was intensified, economic sanctions were instituted, and federal indictments were handed down in Florida. These measures were paralleled by U.S. support of the National Civic Crusade and efforts to promote a palace coup by dissident PDF officers. But psychological operations, economic destabilization, political-opposition building, and CIA plots all failed to topple Noriega. After the flawed coup attempt of October 1989, the Bush administration stepped up plans for a U.S. military invasion.

History of U.S. Intervention

September 19-22, 1856: "To protect U.S. interests during an insurrection."*

September 27 — October 8, 1865: "To protect U.S. interests during a revolution."

April 1868: "To protect the property and lives of U.S. residents during a revolution."

May 7-22 and September 23 — October 9, 1873: "To protect U.S. interests during hostilities caused by the inauguration of the government of Panama."

January 18-19, 1885: "To protect objects of value being moved by Panama's railroad, as well as the Company's safes and vaults during revolutionary activity."

March and April 1885: "To re-establish free transit during revolutionary activity."

March 8-9, 1895: "To protect U.S. interests during an attack on the town of Bocas del Toro by a bandit leader."

November 20 — December 4, 1901: "To protect U.S. lives and property in Bocas del Toro during a civil war."

September 17 — November 18, 1902: "To place armed guards in all crossing trains and maintain the railway open."

1903 — 1914: "With short interruptions, the Marines were stationed in the Isthmus from November 4, 1903 until January 21, 1914 to protect U.S. interests and lives during and following the revolution of independence from Colombia, due to the construction of the canal in the Isthmus."

Four justifications were offered by Washington for the invasion: protection of U.S. lives, promotion of democracy, protection of the canal, and prosecution of Noriega for drug trafficking. Despite the invasion's violation of the charters of the United Nations and Organization of American States, its willful and distorted interpretation of the 1977 Canal Treaties, and its disregard for the War Powers Act, this act of war received wide bipartisan support. It was an invasion by consensus that marked the end to the Vietnam Syndrome.[19]

The December 1989 invasion was a throwback to the era of Gunboat Diplomacy when Washington intervened in the hemisphere to "protect

---

in Panama

November 17-24, 1904: "To protect U.S. lives and property in Ancon, at the time of insurrectionary threat."

1912: "At the request of the political parties, U.S. troops supervised elections outside the Canal Zone."

1918– 1920: "For police duties, according to treaty stipulations, during electoral disturbances and subsequent agitation."

April 1921: "A U.S. Navy squadron held maneuvers on both sides of the Isthmus to prevent war between the two countries [Panama and Costa Rica] over a border dispute."

October 12-23, 1925: "Strikes and riots by tenants obliged some 600 U.S. soldiers to disembark to maintain order and protect U.S. interests."

January 9, 1964: To stop Panamanian students who sought to raise the Panamanian flag in the Canal Zone, U.S. soldiers killed 28 and wounded more than 300 civilians.

March and April 1988: To overthrow the government, the United States imposed devastating economic sanctions.

December 1989: U.S. invades with 26,000 troops to protect U.S. lives and the canal and to restore democracy.

*
Quotes extracted from a list of U.S. interventions in the hemisphere presented in Senate testimony by Secretary of State Dean Rusk in 1962 to justify the option of direct intervention in Cuba.

Sources: Este País Mes a Mes, No. 2, July 1986, CEASPA, Panama; NACLA Report on the Americas, July-August 1988

American lives and property" and to assert the principles of the Monroe Doctrine. But unlike early military invasions and occupations, the new interventionism is, as Latin America analyst Roger Burbach observed, "rooted in the decline of, rather than the ascent of, the U.S. imperial system."[20]

The invasion was unexpectedly costly. According to official U.S. figures, 23 U.S. servicemen were killed and another 324 wounded; three U.S. civilians were killed and one injured; 324 PDF members were killed and another 124 wounded; and 202 Panamanian civilians died.[21] According to the weekly *Panorama Católico*, 655 Panamanians died in the invasion and 2,007 were wounded — most of whom were civilians.[22] The U.S. military, conspicuously silent about the number of civilian deaths, finally reported that a couple hundred had been killed. But unofficial estimates have ranged as high as 4,000. In a visit to Panama to investigate the civilian casualties, former Attorney General Ramsey Clark estimated that at least 1,000 Panamanian civilians had died.

One foreign policy headache was resolved by the invasion but others were immediately created. The invasion was widely condemned throughout Latin America and revived fears of Yankee imperialism. As became obvious soon after the invasion, the arrest of Noriega was not the serious blow to narco-trafficking that Washington promised it to be. In fact, Noriega had largely cleaned up his act in terms of his collaboration with the Medellín Cartel by the mid-1980s and had been cooperating with the Drug Enforcement Administration.[23] Also undermining Washington's case that Noriega was a world-class drug lord were postinvasion revelations that the officials of the new government were connected to banks and individuals involved in the laundering of drug money.[24]

U.S. Trade and Investment

The United States historically has been the country's single most important source of investment and trade. The strong presence of U.S. investment in the Panama predates independence, as U.S. financiers were the majority owners of the Panama Railroad Company. Between 1856 and 1865, the U.S. Army intervened in Panama five times to protect the railroad from possible attacks by Panamanian nationalists.[25]

In the 1970s rightwing defenders of U.S. control of the canal and the Canal Zone predicted that Panamanian nationalism would adversely affect U.S. financial interests in the country. Those predictions, however, proved unfounded. Instead, U.S. investor confidence increased after the signing of the 1977 Canal Treaties. In 1979, the American Society of Panama formed the first American Chamber of Commerce in the country, which within a few years had over 150 sponsoring members.

U.S. trade and investment in Panama was adversely affected by the series of economic sanctions imposed by Washington – measures that have been opposed by the American Chamber of Commerce and other representatives of U.S. traders and investors.[26] Unlike in most Central American countries, U.S. financial interest in Panama is considerable, even by U.S. terms. The book value of U.S. investment in the country was $4.8 billion in 1987 – the third largest in Latin America.[27] According to the American Chamber of Commerce, about one-half of all private-sector business in Panama is U.S.-related.[28] The United States is Panama's single most important trading partner, receiving 60 percent of its exports and supplying 30 percent of its imports.[29] Another factor determining strong U.S. government interest in Panama is the presence of some 40,000 U.S. citizens – both civilian and military – who live and work in the country.[30]

Nature of U.S. Investment

Literally hundreds of U.S. businesses are registered in Panama, but most are only "paper" companies with no operations in Panama. Several such "paper" companies were, for example, established in the mid-1980s by the National Security Council's funding network for the contras.[31] About two-thirds of U.S. investment in Panama is non-productive investment in the offshore banking center.

Nonetheless, U.S. productive investment – amounting to $1.5 billion – still dominates the economy.[32] Six of the top ten U.S. oil companies are active in Panama, one of which – Texaco – owns the country's main oil refinery. United Brands dominates the banana business, and Ralston Purina is the major investor in the seafood industry. Northville Terminal and CBI Industries own the trans-isthmian oil pipeline in a joint venture with the government. General Mills owns a flour mill, and Borden produces dairy products.[33] Until the 1987 political crisis, U.S. firms did exceedingly well in Panama despite the regional turmoil in Central America – enjoying a 20 percent rate of return and pulling in close to $300 million in profits in 1986 alone.[34] In the case of the oil pipeline, finished in 1982, U.S. investors were able to recoup their initial investment in just 18 months. One-third of Alaskan North Slope oil flows through this profitable pipeline.[35]

U.S. Interests Hit Hard by Sanctions

Panamanians and U.S. traders and investors alike suffered from U.S. economic sanctions. (See Economy) The U.S. business sector in Panama charged that the main effect of the sanctions was to drive the U.S. private sector out of the country by placing companies in an untenable situation, financially and legally. "My company has not paid sales taxes, and that can subject me to criminal penalties," one U.S. business complained, "I'm sitting here at Noriega's pleasure. They have every right to throw me in jail."[36] No major U.S. company outside the banking sector pulled up stakes in Panama because of the sanctions. But with U.S. companies hamstrung by economic sanctions, European and Japanese firms began moving in to take their place. Japan's Fuji, for example, rapidly gained ground in market territory once dominated by Kodak.[37]

U.S. Economic Aid

The suspension of U.S. economic aid in 1987 brought to an end a U.S. Agency for International Development (AID) program that averaged some $20 million annually. In itself, the suspension of U.S. economic aid was no great blow to Panama. Between 1980 and 1987, Panama received $139 million in U.S. economic aid. More serious was Washington's decision to use its leverage and vote to block loans to Panama from multilateral institutions like the World Bank and the Inter-American Development Bank. At the same time, the United States also eliminated its sugar quota for Panama, thereby cutting off another source of revenue for the government.

The termination of the U.S. aid program contributed to the U.S. destabilizing strategy of starving the country of cash. It had little impact, however, on the Panamanian poor since most of the AID programs were designed to promote private-sector investment and boost export production. The U.S. food-aid program had been closed down since 1984, and the balance of the programs had little or nothing to do with meeting basic needs or improving socioeconomic conditions.

In 1984 AID launched an economic stabilization program in Panama with Economic Support Funds (ESF). The purpose of this program was to increase the country's financial stability through injections of foreign currency. At the same time, these funds were conditioned on the government's acceptance of policy reforms aimed at decreasing its budget deficit and its role in the economy while bolstering the private sector.[38]

The policy reforms that came with AID's ESF program largely matched the measures imposed by the concurrent International Monetary Fund (IMF) stand-by agreements and the World Bank's structural-adjustment loans. A *Country Development Strategy Statement* drawn up by AID in 1986 noted the "commonalities" of the three assistance programs (IMF, World Bank, and AID) in such areas as the privatization of state enterprises, austerity measures, promotion of agroexports, elimination or reduction of protective tariffs, and removing price supports for basic grains:

AID resources are intended to influence the transition and to contribute to the success of the new policies. Therefore, the strategy [of AID] takes into account the contributions of the other agencies, complements and builds upon their initiatives....We expect that the World Bank and the IMF will continue to take the lead in introducing major structural adjustments. AID will focus its activities on the implementation of those adjustments at the sectoral level [agriculture, industry, government, etc.].[39]

For AID, Panama was a success story. Most of the policy reforms advocated by AID were accepted by the government and duly implemented. Public-sector investment was cut back, state enterprises were sold, austerity measures were implemented, prices were liberalized, and private-sector promotion policies were adopted. This "reform momentum" of structural-adjustment measures also resulted in the "three-in-one" reforms of March 1986, which revised the Labor Code and created new incentives for export production and private-sector investment in the agricultural and industrial sectors.[40]

According to AID, that "reform legislation" set the stage for further economic restructuring and greater reliance on market forces. Changes in the Labor Code "provide incentives for increased productivity at lower costs," while the agricultural reform "will encourage production of commodities for which Panama has a comparative advantage."[41] Labor unions and peasant farmers, however, regarded these measures not as reforms but as gifts to the private-sector elite. "Lower costs" meant lower wages and benefits; and "comparative advantage" meant that small farmers producing grains for the local market had to compete on equal footing with local agribusinesses and foreign suppliers of cheap grains.

AID's Development Assistance and Local Currency programs (funds generated from the sale of ESF dollars on local market) focused on the business sector. These included a technical-assistance program for small businesses, a scholarship fund for business managers, the creation of a new business organization called the National Productivity Council

(CONDEPRO), the funding of two government agencies — Investment Council and the Panamanian Institute for Foreign Commerce — to promote private-sector investment, a $4.5 million project by the Union of Panamanian Industrialists to increase workplace productivity, increased private-sector credit, and a program to create a private-sector policy institute that would allow the private sector "to participate effectively in the dialogue with the government concerning new economic policies."

In the agricultural sector, AID called for "substantial reduction in the support prices for rice, corn, and sorghum," while providing funding and technical assistance to agribusiness projects. While AID did have a program to improve watershed management, mostly out of concern for loss of the canal's watershed, it did not demonstrate great environmental awareness in other areas. In an effort to increase the export of beef, AID financed a meat inspection program, noting that Panama had a comparative advantage in producing grass-fed cattle. Even at current levels, the cattle industry is one of the main causes of deforestation and erosion.[42]

AID's Democratic Initiatives program in Panama sponsored the Central America Peace Scholarships and other education projects which are designed "to expose potential Panamanian leaders to U.S. values, techniques, and institutions and are expected to provide a democratic leaven to Panamanian society." A business youth program planned for 1988 was to "stress the role of democratic processes in the function of a free market." AID also categorized its funding of CONDEPRO and other business associations as "democracy-strengthening" initiatives on the grounds that increased private-sector pressure on government would create a more democratic country.

Also included in AID's democracy strengthening was support for the American Institute for Free Labor Development (AIFLD) and CTRP, its associated confederation in Panama. Through CTRP, AID sponsored population control programs (in conjunction with the Pathfinder Fund), industrial productivity training, and economic and political education courses. While AID mission funding was cut off in December 1987, AID funds still reached Panama through regional and Washington programs, mainly through NGOs. Training and scholarship programs also continued.

AID's Panama Recovery Program

Following the invasion, the Bush administration immediately moved to provide substantial economic support for the new government. The major elements of this $1 billion in planned assistance were to be disaster relief, trade credits, support for the private sector, balance-of-payments support, immediate debt relief, aid for a public-sector restructuring and investment program, and an emergency public-sector employment program. On announcing the aid package, Bush stressed that "Private-sector initiatives, supported by the government's economic reform policies, will be the key to Panama's recovery, enabling the entrepreneurial talents of the Panamanian people to flourish."[43]

An immediate $1 million in disaster relief for feeding programs, rubble removal, and temporary shelter for the displaced was sent to Panama following the invasion. This was to be supplemented by $42 million in humanitarian assistance, including funds for replacement housing for El Chorrillo residents, an emergency public works program, small business rehabilitation assistance, and technical assistance to the government. In addition, the Defense Department facilitated the transport and delivery of U.S. private humanitarian aid.

Close to $500 million in aid was announced in loans, guarantees, and export assistance "to strengthen Panama's private sector and create jobs." This included up to $400 million in trade guarantees for U.S. exporters to Panama through the Export-Import Bank and the affiliated Foreign Credit Insurance Association. AID was authorized to use $15 million in Trade Credit Insurance Program funds to support additional U.S. lending to private-sector borrowers. The Overseas Private Insurance Corporation (OPIC) was told to reopen its programs to back U.S. foreign investment in Panama.

The U.S. Department of Agriculture will pitch in with $15 million in PL480 Title I food assistance and a $15 million Commodity Credit Program. Bush also told the U.S. Trade Representative to restore the country's suspended 1990 sugar quota and to compensate it for its foregone 1989 quota — together worth $28 million.

Another $500 million was requested by the Bush administration in Economic Support Funds (ESF), consisting of the following components: $185 million in balance-of-payments/business credit funds, a $145 million public investment program, $20 million for public sector restructuring, $20 million for private-sector export promotion and watershed protection for the canal, and $130 million to help erase over $540 million in debt payment arrears.

Although part of the aid package is designed to provide immediate humanitarian relief and temporary jobs, the main thrust of the recovery aid is to stabilize the government by helping it meet its high debt payments and to support the country's business sector with credit and export promotion programs. According to AID, the large injection of U.S. aid is "necessary to jump-start the economy and help Panama regularize the relations with external creditors."[44] Despite early promises from the White House and Congress, congressional budget constraints and a rising chorus of demand for U.S. aid by Eastern European countries and Nicaragua reduced the chances that Panama would be receiving the full $500 million in direct economic aid for 1990.

U.S. Military Presence

U.S. military intervention in Panama dates back to the mid-1800s when U.S. troops provided security for the U.S.-owned railroad that traversed the country. This protective role expanded in the early 1900s to include the canal, built by the U.S. Army Corps of Engineers, and the new U.S. corporate and commercial investments in Panama, including the banana plantations of the United Fruit Company.

This military mission of protecting U.S. lives, investment, and national interests in Panama quickly broadened to include intervention in the country's internal political affairs. Although not officially a U.S. protectorate, Panama was for the first half of this decade treated much like a colony. Troops stationed in the Canal Zone broke local strikes, repressed political dissidents, and supervised elections.

For many observers the 1977 Canal Treaties were seen as a decisive turning point in the U.S. military mission in Panama. The treaty relating to the neutrality of the canal stipulated that U.S. troops had no right to intervene in Panama's internal affairs and that they would leave Panamanian soil by the year 2000. It was further agreed that certain U.S. military facilities would be turned over to the Panamanian military which would assume increased responsibility for the defense of the canal.

Instead of the gradual reduction in U.S. military presence in Panama that many had expected, U.S. military operations expanded and intensified during the 1980s. Although there were some cutbacks — notably the transfer of the U.S. Army School of the Americas to Ft. Benning, Georgia — all other signs pointed to the increased use and importance of the U.S. military infrastructure in Panama.

When the canal treaties were signed in 1977 the Panama-based U.S. Southern Command (SOUTHCOM) was the least important of the four regional commands. The Pentagon saw no pressing security threats in Latin America and was considering closing this sleepy tropical command. Political upheaval in Central America and the formation of a revolutionary government in Grenada during the first half of the decade and U.S. military intervention in Peru, Bolivia, and Colombia in the late 1980s dramatically increased the strategic importance of the Southern Command.

Military strategists pointed to turmoil in the region—popular rebellion, the rise of leftist guerrilla armies, and new prominence of drug trafficking—as confirmation of the changing focus of U.S. military doctrine away from conventional high-intensity warfare toward low-intensity conflicts (LIC) in the third world. Central America was regarded as a laboratory for evolving counterinsurgency theory and tactics, and South America as a proving ground for the new LIC emphasis on counterterrorism and anti-drug operations. As if overnight, SOUTHCOM changed from a sleepy command to one responsible for a region of "high probability conflict."[45]

SOUTHCOM suddenly buzzed with activity—providing intelligence for the Salvadoran military, training and coordinating the contras, and directing frequent military maneuvers. An estimated 50 intelligence-gathering sites had been established in Panama, and from Howard Air Force Base the CIA and National Security Agency launched high-altitude espionage missions over Nicaragua and El Salvador.[46]

Defending the canal had become a minor part of its mission. Although most of this stepped-up military operations were hidden from public view, SOUTHCOM also made its might more immediately visible outside its military bases through large-scale military maneuvers and civic-action programs throughout the country.

SOUTHCOM: A Home in Panama

The U.S. Southern Command (SOUTHCOM) is one of four regional U.S. military commands in the world—the others being the Atlantic Command, Pacific Command, and European Command. The smallest of the these commands, SOUTHCOM is responsible for U.S. military activities in Central and South America.[47] It defines its mission as the following:

* Operational command over U.S. forces in the region.

* Safeguard U.S. access to raw materials and energy resources.

* Conduct operations for disaster relief, search and rescue, and evacuation of U.S. citizens from endangered areas.

* Conduct training and military operations.

* Counter international terrorism, subversion, and illegal trafficking of arms and drugs.

* Fulfill mutual security pacts between Washington and Latin American nations.[48]

Prior to the December 1989 invasion approximately 11,000 U.S. troops were permanently stationed in Panama. In addition, SOUTH-COM employed 8,600 civilian employees, 70 percent of these workers being Panamanian. Under the provisions of the Treaty on the Permanent Neutrality and Operation of the Panama Canal, all U.S. military personnel must leave the country by the year 2000 unless separate agreements are reached. Immediately following the ratification of the canal treaties, several U.S. military facilities were handed over to Panama while other facilities were designated Military Areas of Coordination for joint U.S.-

---

Treaty-Mandated Transfers or Changes in Military Facilities

The following facilities were transferred to Panama (1979-1984):

* Portion of U.S. Army facilities at Fort Amador, including 17 office buildings and 8 housing complexes.
* The hangars and runway at the Albrook Army Airfield—but not affecting the contiguous Albrook Air Force Station.
* Panama Air Depot buildings.
* Twenty housing units at Curundu Heights.
* Troop buildings and barracks at Fort Gulick including those housing the U.S. Army School of the Americas which was later renamed Fuerte José Domingo Espinar by the Panamanian military.

The following facilities were designated Military Areas of Coordination:

* Quarry Heights—site of SOUTHCOM offices.
* The naval part of Fort Amador.
* Housing facilities at Fort Amador and Fort Gulick and at Curundu and Coco Solo South.
* Training areas including Empire and Pina Ranges, Fort Sherman West, and Fort Clayton Training Area.
* Numerous special schooling, communications, and health facilities.

Panamanian use. (See Box) The following facilities were designated Defense Sites under the exclusive control of the U.S. military until 2000:[49]

* Fort Clayton (including Corozal Military Reservation).

* Fort Davis (including Dock 45).

* Fort Sherman.

* Fort Kobbe/Howard Air Force Base (including the Farfan Naval Area).

* U.S. Naval Station at Rodman.

* Marine Barracks.

* Albrook Air Force Station.

* Galeta Island.

* U.S. Navy Transisthmian Pipeline.

* Atlantic General Depot Area.

* Semaphore Hill radar and communications site.

SOUTHCOM is composed of components of three branches of the armed forces (Army, Navy, Air Force), a special command in Honduras, security assistance operations for Latin America, and the Special Operations Command South. In addition, the U.S. military facilities in Panama host a wide range of military and intelligence operations not directly under SOUTHCOM authority.

The **U.S. Army South,** by far the largest of SOUTHCOM's components, was formed in 1986 after the redesignation and restructuring of the 193rd Infantry Brigade. Headquartered at Fort Clayton, this large army unit also operates Fort Kobbe, Fort David, and Fort Sherman. It has 7,000 assigned personnel including 4,200 combat troops. Among the responsibilities assigned to the U.S. Army South in Panama are the following:

* Command of the 193rd Infantry Brigade (Light) which is responsible for ground defense of the canal. Other smaller units under U.S. Army South command are the 324th Support Group, 1st Battalion, 228th Aviation Regiment, 470th Military Intelligence Brigade, Military Police Command, and 41st Area Support Group.

* Commanding general of Army South heads the U.S. Army Security Agency Latin America, located at Fort Clayton.

* Training of affiliated reserve component units including the 92nd Infantry Brigade of Puerto Rican Army National Guard.

* Support of LIC doctrine development and equipment.

Numerous U.S. Army and Department of Defense units and agencies are housed on U.S. Army South facilities in Panama, the most important of which are:

* 1109th U.S. Army Signal Brigade.

* U.S. Army Security Assistance Agency Latin America. This office manages security assistance programs including Foreign Military Sales (FMS) and the International Military Education and Training (IMET) programs.

* U.S. Army Tropic Test Center.

* Third Battalion, 7th Special Forces Group (Airborne).

* U.S. Army Medical Department Activity.

* Jungle Operations Training Center.

* Defense Mapping Agency/Inter-American Geodetic Survey.

* U.S. Army Troop Support Agency.

* Department of Defense Dependents Schools.

The **U.S. Air Force Component** is the 830th Air Division located at the Albrook Air Force Station. The 830th, a Tactical Air Command unit, is a division of the 12th Air Force at Bergstrom Air Force Base in Texas. Located at Howard Air Force Base, SOUTHCOM's air component, which has 2,400 personnel, has operational control of C-130 Hercules, A-7D Corsair II, and A-37 Dragonfly aircraft. Its missions in Panama include:

* Air defense of the Panama Canal.

* Air support for military maneuvers.

The **U.S. Naval Component** of SOUTHCOM coordinates all U.S. naval activities in Panama from its headquarters at Fort Amador, including the following:

* U.S. Naval Small Craft and Technical Training School.

* Military Sealift Command.

* Regional U.S. Naval Oceanographic Office.

* Naval Security Group Activity (Galeta Island).

* Inter-American Naval Telecommunications Network.

Two other components are the **Special Operations Command** at Albrook Air Force Base and the **Joint Task Force-Bravo** which is headquartered in Honduras. In addition, SOUTHCOM administers 16 Security Assistance Organizations (SAOs) throughout Latin America. These SAOs include all the U.S. military personnel assigned to the U.S.

embassies and national military commands, including the military assistance advisory groups (MAAG), military groups (USMILGP), military liaison officers (MLO), offices of defense cooperation (ODC), and defense attache personnel.

SOUTHCOM administers the U.S. military's security assistance program in the region. Mobile Training Teams (MTTs), based in Panama, travel to other Latin American and Caribbean countries to train armies in the use of U.S. military equipment. The U.S. Military Groups that advise U.S. embassies and Latin American governments and military high commands are also administered by SOUTHCOM.

U.S. Military Aid and Training

Historically the United States has exercised major influence and control over the Panamanian security forces. In 1904 U.S. military authorities dissolved the Panamanian army and ten years later disarmed the police forces. Beginning in the 1940s, however, the Panamanian police were given increased autonomy and U.S. training and support.

Most important among U.S. programs was the U.S. Army School of the Americas. Over 5,000 members of the Panamanian National Guard were trained at the school before it was relocated to Ft. Benning, Georgia in 1984. Instruction in jungle warfare, intelligence operations, counterinsurgency and psychological operations was made available to National Guard officers at other Canal Area training facilities. Among those who received this training were Omar Torrijos and his two successors, Rubén Darío Paredes and Manuel Noriega.

Although the National Guard relied on the U.S. military for training and supplies, the level of U.S. support was relatively small before 1979. Between 1946 and 1979 Panama received $13 million in U.S. supplies and training. Between 1980 and 1987, however, the level of U.S. support increased steadily. During that period Panama received $47.3 million in U.S. military aid and training. In addition, the Panamanian military also became a favored recipient of surplus U.S. military equipment and participated in annual joint military maneuvers with the United States. The National Guard/PDF also benefited from the transfer of U.S. military property and the use of coordinated military areas as mandated by agreements associated with the canal treaties.[50]

The evolution of the National Guard from a police force into an army responsible for defending the canal and handling the growing regional turmoil was the reason for this increased military support after 1979. The Reagan administration was interested in shaping the National Guard into a strong allied force capable not only of protecting the canal, but also in backing the aggressive U.S. military policy in Central America.

The treaties prompted closer cooperation between the U.S. military and the Panamanian National Guard. Washington promised Panama $50 million in military aid in the decade following the treaties.

SOUTHCOM organized a series of joint military maneuvers "to test and evaluate mutual capabilities in the mission of defense of the Panama Canal" and to prepare the PDF for its defense responsibility as the first-line defender of the canal. In coordination with the PDF, SOUTHCOM also initiated wide-ranging civic-action programs involving road construction and medical care. During the 1980s these civic-action programs involved the largest concentration of noncombat U.S. troops in Latin America, with the exception of Honduras.

Future of SOUTHCOM

According to the 1977 Canal Treaties, SOUTHCOM has to be out of the country by the first day of the year 2000. There has been much speculation about a possible relocation site for SOUTHCOM. Honduras has been mentioned as one possibility but most military experts consider this unlikely. Other sites mentioned include Patrick Air Force Base and Mac-Dill Air Force Base in Florida; Fort Polk and the New Orleans Naval Air Station in Louisiana; and Brooks Air Force Base and Fort Sam Houston in San Antonio, Texas.[51]

In late 1988 the Department of Defense announced a preliminary proposal for the "orderly phased withdrawal" of all U.S. troops from Panama. This Treaty Implementation Plan, apparently drawn up as a contingency plan in the face of growing instability in Panama, specified no sites for the relocation but noted that SOUTHCOM would continue as a unified regional command beyond the end of the century.[52] After leaving their posts, the last four SOUTHCOM commanders have all called for SOUTHCOM's relocation.

Although SOUTHCOM will probably be relocating in the 1990s, there is little likelihood that the United States will close all its military bases in Panama. To keep a military presence in Panama, however, the United States will have to renegotiate the 1977 Canal Treaties to give it the right to maintain bases into the next decade. It is also possible that a separate agreement between Panama and the United States will be drawn up allowing the bases to remain in exchange for a annual fee, similar to arrangements in Spain and the Philippines.

A High-Tech Invasion

The Seismology Station of the University of Panama reported 422 explosions in Panama City from just before 1 a.m. on the morning of December 20 to 13 hours later when its monitors broke down. This amounted to a bomb every two minutes in the capital, not counting the explosions in Colón and in the interior of the country.[53]

The U.S. invasion was a well-planned, high-tech venture that had the distinct advantage of being an inside job. Unlike earlier U.S. invasions of Grenada and the Dominican Republic, the U.S. forces were already in the country and had been planning the takeover for at least several months. To avoid the communications fiasco of Grenada in 1983, a joint operation of the armed forces, the U.S. Marines led the occupation of December 1989.

In line with Low Intensity Conflict doctrine, Operation Just Cause was to be a quick-strike mission designed to avoid the loss of U.S. lives. The U.S. military used the opportunity to try out some of its newest technology and combat gear. The billion-dollar super-secret F-11A Stealth was used to bomb the PDF's headquarters. Also used against the PDF were the night-flying AH-64 Apache attack helicopters and the new HMMWV jeeps. The latest in bullet-proof vests and helmets, as well as the military's new semi-dry rations, were also tested in Panama.[54]

Following the invasion U.S. troops became an occupying force, taking up police and judicial functions and arresting hundreds of suspected Noriega supporters and collaborators. Hundreds of specialists in psychological operations (PSYOPS) were immediately put to work to "bolster the image of the United States" and "to stamp American influence on almost every phase of the new government."[55] Military aid once again began flowing to Panama to reconstitute the country's police and military forces. Some $9 million in redirected military aid was approved for the new Panamanian Public Forces (PPF).

Other Foreign Interests

Traditionally a U.S. enclave, Panama in the last two decades has become a magnet for other foreign investors and traders, particularly those from the Pacific Rim. Like the United States, the Asian nations, led by Japan, have been drawn to Panama by its ready access to international markets, its favorable business climate, and its political stability. In addition, Asian nations regard Panama as a convenient export platform to the United States and South America. The International Financial Center and the Colón Free Zone are focal points for much of this new foreign interest in Panama.

Japan Becomes Major Player

Over the last decade Japan made a dramatic entry into the world of trade, investment, and finance in Panama. This is the result of Japan's rising commercial interests in the whole of Latin America. It also reflects Japan's recognition of the increasing significance of the Panama Canal to its expanding trade in the Western Hemisphere and its post-1977 concern over the future of the canal. With its pervasive U.S. presence, Panama represents for Japan a stable and political tranquil market in this tumultuous region.[56]

In 1988 Japan accounted for one-fourth of the total cargo transiting the canal. The waterway has become vital for certain Japanese industries: nearly 60 percent of the country's vehicle exports to the U.S. east coast pass through the canal and about 50 percent of the country's grain imports are shipped through the canal.[57] Japan's concern over the canal's future is reflected in its participation (with Panama and the United States) in the tripartite Commission for the Study of Alternatives for the Panama Canal. This commission is analyzing the feasibility of a sea-level canal, a larger lock system, and a nonhydraulic complementary system for transisthmian transit. In addition, Tokyo has offered to spend $400 million to widen the canal to make it accessible to larger ships. As former President Erick Arturo Delvalle observed in 1985, Japan is "more than willing to finance the whole thing [enlargement of the canal] 100 percent."[58]

Paralleling Japan's increasing dependence on the canal has been the country's expanding trade and investment in Panama. By early 1987, Japanese investment reached $11.1 billion, making Panama the second-largest recipient (following the United States) of Japanese investment.[59] The bulk of this investment was tied up in Panama's international service economy rather in direct productive investment. Panama-registered Japanese ships accounted for the major portion of this paper investment followed by Japanese investment in the banking sector. In 1987, over 40 Japanese-operated financial service institutions were registered in Panama.[60]

Japan is the principal user of the Colón Free Zone, mostly as a distribution center for its exports to Latin America. Japanese products accounted for some 25 percent of the roughly $2 billion in goods that passed through the Free Zone in 1987. In the last decade, Panama and Japan have become important trading partners. Only the United States surpasses Japan in the volume of goods exported to Panama.

As the stability that attracted Japan to Panama has faded, so has a large part of Japan's involvement in the country's financial service economy. Reacting swiftly to the political turmoil, Japan divested over $3 million in 1988. During the height of the crisis, only one Japanese bank, the Bank of Tokyo, continued to offer a complete line of services while other banks dramatically cut back on staff and services. Yet Japanese participation in the Colón Free Zone has remained strong as has the country's interest in future of the Panama Canal. It seems certain that Japan remains committed to maintaining its commercial beachhead in Panama and playing a major role in evolution of the canal.

Taiwan and the Soviet Union

Japan has not been alone among Asian nations in recognizing the value of Panama as a doorway to Western Hemisphere markets. Among the other countries that have increased their financial stake in Panama are Taiwan, South Korea, China, Singapore, and Hong Kong. Of these nations, Taiwan has developed the most extensive ties to Panama. This is partly explained by the fact that Panama harbors the largest per capita Chinese community within the hemisphere, which exerts a steady, pro-Taiwan pressure.

The Taiwanese government itself has concentrated on Panama as a focal point for its drive to expand trade in Latin America and to shut out its arch-rival and neighbor, the Peoples' Republic of China, from similar opportunities. Taiwan ranks second behind Japan in its presence in the Colón Free Zone. In 1988, Taiwan also proposed creating an all-Taiwanese export-processing zone (EPZ) in Panama, which would use the country as an platform from which to export goods to Latin America and into the United States under the provisions of the Caribbean Basin Initiative (CBI).[61] These plans were put on hold during the political crisis but took on a renewed life in 1990. One clear sign, however, that the political instability of Panama was discouraging new Taiwanese ventures was the decision by Evergreen Marine, the island nation's major shipping line, to locate its regional headquarters in Jamaica, not in Panama as originally planned.[62]

Panama is Taiwan's most important diplomatic representation in the Western Hemisphere. When Panama's relations with the United States worsened in mid-1987, Taiwan appointed as their ambassador the former Strategic Adviser to Taiwan's president to help the country move through the diplomatic mine field. Taiwan was also a favorite training area for PDF officers and an important supplier of arms and military equipment.

The Soviet Union does not even enjoy diplomatic relations with Panama but it has been consistently very supportive of Panamanian efforts to win more control over the canal. During the Torrijos era, Panama was regarded as an exemplary case of a "patriotic military regime." Together with the People's Party of Panama (the official communist party), the Soviet Union applauded all efforts to assert its sovereignty in opposition to Washington, although the Soviet Union has never directly challenged U.S. hegemony in Panama.[63]

Panama, while never shunning Soviet initiatives, has been extremely cautious in its response for fear of needlessly antagonizing the United States. A trade agreement between the two countries which had been written in 1979 was finally signed in 1988, and is regarded as the first step toward establishing diplomatic relations. One sign of increased Soviet interest in Panama and its expanding commercial interests with the country is the presence in the Colón Free Zone of a Soviet manufacturing and distribution center that assembles cars, watches, and clocks for export. Under the new trade agreement, the import of Soviet fertilizers and agricultural products may increase. Although the dollar value of bilateral trade is still small, the political implications of the warming relations may prove to be significant in future U.S.-Panama negotiations.

Israeli Arms Dealing

At the same time that Panama was becoming a principal target for expanding Asian trade and investment, it also became a platform for the expanding Israeli arms trade. Through Panama, Israeli arms dealers gained access to other Latin American countries, particularly those of Central America. The Panama-Israeli arms connection was revealed in the wake of the Iran-Contra scandal. Its key figure has been Mike Harari, a former Mossad (Israeli intelligence) agent who developed close ties with Torrijos and later with Noriega.[64]

As an adviser to Noriega, Harari helped train elements of an elite 100-member Panamanian antiterrorist force called UESAT, which, among other functions, served as a personal security force for Noriega.[65] He also served as the key contact person for secret Israeli operations involving the funneling of Israeli arms and technology into Central America. According to *Israeli Foreign Affairs*, Harari's name also turned up in the unraveling of the covert U.S.-Israeli contra support network. The former Mossad officer apparently had also forged links with the Medellín Cartel, helping to deliver cocaine to the United States and in turn diverting drug profits to the contras.

Shortly after the botched October 1989 coup, Harari took over the day-to-day operations of the PDF's intelligence operations. He replaced Col Guillermo Wong after Wong was arrested following the failed coup d'etat.[66] Despite protestations by the Bush administration, Israel declined to call Harari home, claiming that he is a private citizen.[67] Shortly after the invasion, Harari was back in Israel and the Israeli government let it be known that he would not be subject to extradition because of his knowledge of "sensitive state secrets." Just six hours before the invasion, an Israeli C-130 cargo aircraft took off from Panama, presumably with personnel and files detailing Israeli operations in the country. It is possible that Harari was on that plane but U.S. military reports that he was being held for interrogation indicate that Harari may not have left until a few days after the invasion was underway.[68]

Reference Notes

Introduction

1. "Panama: Ever the Crossroads," *National Geographic*, April 1986.
2. John Weeks, "Panama: The Roots of Current Political Stability," *Third World Quarterly*, July 1987, p. 764.

Chapter One

1. In 1904, 1908, 1912, and 1916, the head of government was chosen by an electoral college. From 1920 to 1968 there was direct popular vote every four years. In 1972 and 1978, the presidential elections were conducted by the National Assembly. In 1984 the country returned to direct presidential vote. Marco A. Gandásegui, "La Democracia en Panamá," *Estudios Sociales Centroamericanos*, May-August 1988.
2. "Interview with Xabier Gorostiaga," *CEPAD Report*, September-October 1989.
3. George Priestley, *Military Government and Popular Participation in Panama: The Torrijos Regime, 1968-1975* (Boulder: Westview Press, 1986), p. 11.
4. Ibid.
5. John Weeks, "Of Puppets and Heroes," *NACLA Report on the Americas*, July-August 1988, p. 13.
6. A Costa Rican judicial investigation concluded in a December 1989 report that a drug and arms trafficking network including CIA operatives working with Lt. Col. Oliver North, Costa Rican officials, and Gen. Manuel Noriega was responsible for the 1984 press conference bombing at La Penca, Nicaragua which killed three journalists. The report also recommended the indictment of Lt. Col. Luis Cordova, a close Noriega associate, for the 1985 murder of Dr. Hugo Spadafora, who was a contra associate of Eden Pastora, the

target of the 1985 bombing. Shortly before his murder, Spadafora told pilots working for Noriega as part of this drug and arms network that he intended to expose the general's drug trafficking. *Public Prosecutors Investigation of "La Penca" Case* (San José: Costa Rica Department of Justice, December 26, 1989).

7. In addition to the use of the term *rabiblancos* Panamanians also use *rabiprietos (mestizos)* and *rabicolorados* (blacks).

8. For a revealing look at the overlap between the country's political parties and business organizations see: Juana Camargo, "Los Partidos Políticos y los Gremios Empresiarles en la Conyuntura Actual," *Revista Panameña de Sociología*, No. 5 (Universidad de Panamá, Departamento de Sociología, 1989).

9. Sharon Phillipps, "Labor Policy in an Inclusionary-Authoritarian Regime: Panama Under Torrijos," Dissertation (University of New Mexico, July 1987), pp. 26-28.

10. John Weeks, "Panama: The Roots of Current Political Instability," *Third World Quarterly*, July 1987, p. 769.

11. Arias was inaugurated president in 1940, 1949, and 1968. He was denied the presidency in the fraudulent elections of 1964 and 1984.

12. Milciades Pinzón Rodríguez, "Arnulfo Arias Madrid: Populismo y Mesianismo," *Diálogo Social*, September 1988.

13. CONEP, *En Pocas Palabras, Esto Es CONEP* (Panama: n.d.), cited by Phillipps, op. cit., p. 26.

14. Phillipps, op. cit., p. 45.

15. Ibid., p. 47.

16. For a discussion of the crisis of hegemony in Panamanian politics between 1968 and 1984 see: Marco A. Gandásegui, "Militares y Crisis de los Partidos Políticos," *Tareas*, No. 66, June-September 1987.

17. The first National Guard commander, José Antonio Remón Cantera (1943-1952), was an impoverished cousin of the Chiari family. His successor, Bolívar Vallarino (1952-1968), was a member of an important pre-independence family.

18. Renato Pereira, *Panamá: Fuerzas Armadas y Política* (Panama City: Ediciones Nueva Universidad, 1979), p. 136-145.

19. Raúl Leis, "Cousins' Republic," *NACLA Report on the Americas*, July-August 1988, p. 24.

20. Phillipps, op. cit., p. 63; Robert Howard Miller, "Military Government and Approaches to National Development," Dissertation (Miami: University of Miami, 1975).

21. Gandásegui, "Militares y Crisis," op. cit.

22. Phillipps, op. cit., p. 57.

23. José Sossa, *Imperialismos: Fuerzas Armadas y Partidos Políticos en Panamá* (Panama City: Ediciones Documentos, 1977), cited in Phillipps, op. cit., p. 58.

24. Gandásegui, "Militares y Crisis," op. cit., p. 30.

25. Unlike the National Assembly of 1972, the one of 1989 was appointed not elected. Like the 1972-1978 period, Panama had both a president and head of government. The president from 1972 to 1978 was Demetrio Lakas.

26. Priestley, op. cit., p.56.

27. Phillipps, op. cit., p. 107.

28. Priestley, op. cit., pp. 36-50.

29. Ibid., p. 120.

30. Ibid.

31. Gandásegui, "Militares y Crisis," op. cit.

32. Brook Larmer, "Noriega Pulls Election Strings" *Christian Science Monitor*, April 12, 1989.

33. John M. Zindar, "Opposition Outflanked," *NACLA Report on the Americas*, July-August 1988.

34. Raúl Leis, "Diez Ideas Sobre el Panamá de Hoy," *Este País Mes a Mes*, February 1990, p. 19.

35. Leis, "Cousins' Republic," op. cit, p. 26.

36. Joaquín Ortega, " La Izquierda Buscando Alternativa," *Opinión Pública*, 1988, p. 4.

37. *New York Times*, November 27, 1987.

38. Internal National Security Council memorandum, October 30, 1984, cited in Jim Morrel and William Goodfellow, "Contadora: Under the Gun," *International Policy Report*, May 1986.

39. Amnesty International, *Amnesty International Report 1988*.

40. *Central America Report*, March 31, 1989.

41. *The Reagan Administration's Record on Human Rights in 1988* (Human Rights Watch and Lawyers Committee for Human Rights, January 1989), pp. 136-37.

Chapter Two

1. U.S. Embassy, *Panama Defense Forces*, Information handout (1989).
2. Kenneth Jones, ed., *Panama Now* (Panama City: Focus Publications, 1986), p. 21.
3. U.S. Embassy, *Panama Defense Forces*, op. cit.
4. See Steve Ropp, *Panamanian Politics: From Guarded Nation to National Guard* (New York: Praeger, 1982). Also see the following essays in *Revista Panameña de Sociología*, No. 5 (Universidad de Panamá, Departamento de Sociología): Marco A. Gandásegui, "Las FDP y el Año 2000;" Renato Pereira, "Fuerzas Armadas y Partidos Políticos;" Everardo Bósquez De León, "Fuerzas de Defensa y el Año 2000."
5. Marco A. Gandásegui, *Panamá: Crisis Política y Agresión Económica* (Panama City: CELA, 1989), p. 16.
6. George Priestley, *Military Government and Popular Participation in Panama: The Torrijos Regime, 1968-1975* (Boulder: Westview Press, 1986).
7. Alfonso Villarreal, "Fuerzas Armadas de Panamá: Aspectos Históricos, Políticos, y Jurídicos de la Ley No. 20," in *Revista Panameña de Sociología*, No. 5 (Universidad de Panamá, Departamento de Sociología).
8. U.S. Embassy, *Panama Defense Forces* op. cit.
9. *Latin American Weekly Report*, October 19, 1989.
10. *Latin American Weekly Report*, October 26, 1989.
11. Council on Hemispheric Affairs, *Survey of Press Freedom in Latin America 1985-1986* (Washington: COHA, December 1986), p. 45.
12. Andres Oppenheimer, "Noriega's Next Move in Doubt," *Miami Herald*, May 12, 1989.

Chapter Three

1. Raúl Leis, "Diez Ideas Sobre el Panama de Hoy," *Este País Mes a Mes*, February 1990.
2. For a description of the Panamanian oligarchy see: Marco A. Gandásegui, "La Concentración del Poder Económico en Panamá," *Tareas,* No. 18, 1967; and William R. Hughes and Ivan A. Quintero, *¿Quiénes Son los Dueños de Panama?* (Panama City: CEASPA, 1987).

3. Marco A. Gandásegui and George Priestley, "Panama: Political Crisis and Economic Aggression," *Central America Bulletin*, Vol. 8, No. 3.

4. Ibid.

5. Omar Torrijos, *La Batalla de Panamá* (Buenos Aires, 1973), p. 111, as cited in George Priestley, *Military Government and Popular Participation in Panama: The Torrijos Regime, 1968-1975* (Boulder: Westview Press, 1986), p. 57.

6. Gandásegui and Priestley, "Panama: Political Crisis," op. cit.

7. Cited in Priestley, *Military Government*, op. cit., p. 65.

8. Ibid., p. 119.

9. The month before, National Security Adviser John Poindexter had traveled to Panama to communicate U.S. policy concerning drug smuggling and internal politics. At the same time, Noriega apparently tried to strike a deal to offer to do more to support U.S. foreign policy in Central America in return for an end to U.S. pressure.

10. Agency for International Development, *U.S. Overseas Loans and Grants: Obligations and Loan Authorizations, July 1, 1945-September 30, 1987* (Washington: AID, 1989).

11. Mark Sullivan, "Panama: Dilemma for U.S. Policy," *CRS Review*, February 1989, p. 21.

12. Ibid.

13. The informal sector of the economy rose from 28.4 percent in 1987 to 35.6 percent a year later.

14. *Washington Report on the Hemisphere*, March 15, 1989, quoting Michael May, spokesperson of the American Chamber of Commerce.

15. Gary Clyde Hufbayer and Jeffrey Schott, *Economic Sanctions in Support of Foreign Policy Goals* (Washington: Institute for International Economics, 1983).

16. Charlotte Elton, "Serving Foreigners," *NACLA Report on the Americas*, July-August 1988, p. 30.

17. Ibid., p. 29.

18. *Central America Report*, January 26, 1990.

19. U.S. Embassy, *Foreign Economic Trends* (Washington: Department of Commerce, August 1988).

20. *Este País Mes a Mes*, February 1989.

21. H. Jeffrey Leonard, *Natural Resources and Economic Development in Central America* (New Brunswick, NJ: Transaction Books, 1987), pp. 4, 16.

22. Ibid., pp. 18, 222.

23. Tom Barry, *Roots of Rebellion: Land and Hunger in Central America* (Boston: South End Press, 1987), p. 9; *Centro América 1988* (Guatemala City: Inforpress Centroamericana, 1989), pp. 235-236.

24. Agency for International Development, *Panama: Country Development Strategy Statement FY1988-1992* (Washington: AID, February 1986), p. 15.

25. George Priestley, *Military Government and Popular Participation in Panama: The Torrijos Regime, 1968-1975* (Boulder: Westview Press, 1986), p. 55. The information for this section on Torrijos and the peasantry is taken largely from this study.

26. Ibid., p. 56.

27. Ibid., p. 63.

28. Ibid., p. 60.

29. Economic Intelligence Unit, *Country Profile: Panama, 1988-1989*, p. 56.

30. The country's extremely wet tropical climate is not ideal for sugar cane, and results in cane which has a low sugar content and high refining costs.

31. During the 1980s traditional agricultural and industrial exports (bananas, coffee, refined petroleum, sugar, clothing, and fish meal) experienced a $40 million decline.

32. Kenneth Jones, ed., *Panama Now* (Panama City: Focus Publications, 1986), p. 61.

33. Elton, "Serving Foreigners," op. cit.; *Panama Now*, op. cit., p. 62.

34. Figure from the Panamanian Tourist Institute, 1982.

35. *New York Times*, February 6, 1989.

36. Stephen Labaton, "Panama Is Resisting U.S. Pressure," *New York Times*, February 6, 1990.

37. Elton, "Serving Foreigners," op. cit., p. 28.

38. Ibid.

39. Panama Petroterminal is a joint venture with the government holding 40 percent, Northville Industries with 38.75 percent, and Chicago Bridge and Iron with 21.25 percent.

40. Elton, "Serving Foreigners," op. cit., p. 28.

41. *Panama Now*, op. cit., p. 80.

42. *Business Latin America*, February 6, 1989.

43. *Revista Panameña de Sociología,* No. 3 (Universidad de Panama, Departamento de Sociología).

44. The average rates of tariff protection have been below those imposed by the members of the Central America Common Market but Panama has also protected local industry with extensive import quotas. These quotas were often imposed by the government at the request of well-connected manufacturers. Andrew Zimbalist, "Panama," in *Struggle Against Dependence: Nontraditional Export Growth in Central America and the Caribbean* (Boulder: Westview Press, 1988), pp. 86-87.

45. Ibid.

Chapter Four

1. Didimo Castillo, "Movimientos Sociales Urbanos y Democracia: El Caso de Panamá, *Revista Panameña de Sociología*, No. 5 (Universidad de Panamá, Departamento de Sociología).

2. Raúl Leis, "Cuatro Ideas Sobre el Papel de Los Sectores Populares en la Coyuntura Actual," *Este País Mes a Mes*, October 1987.

3. Interview by Debra Preusch, March 28, 1989.

4. Lucía Luna, "La Clara Intervención Estadunidense, Dirigida Contra el Grupo de Los Ocho," *Proceso* (Mexico), March 7, 1988.

5. James Aparicio, "Las Barriadas Brujas," *Diálogo Social*, October 1986.

6. Virgilio Hernández, "El Más Jóven Distrito," *Diálogo Social*, January 1986.

7. Leis, "Cuatro Ideas Sobre el Papel de Los Sectores Populares," op. cit.

8. John Zindar, "Opposition Outflanked," *NACLA Report on the Americas*, July-August 1988.

9. Lindsey Gruson, "Oligarchs and Soldiers, Glaring Across Battle Line," *New York Times*, May 4, 1989.

10. Frederick Kempe, "Most Panamanians Stop Waiting for U.S. Godot," *Wall Street Journal*, October 13, 1989.

11. Raúl Leis, "Diez Ideas Sobre el Panamá de Hoy," *Este País Mes a Mes*, February 1990.

12. *CIA World Factbook* (1988); U.S. Embassy, *Foreign Labor Trends: Panama* (Department of Labor, 1986).

13. *CIA World Factbook* (1988); *Business Latin America*, January 23, 1989.

14. Two important sources on labor movement history are: Andrés Achong, *Orígines del Movimiento Obrero Panameño* (Panama City: CELA, 1980) and Marco A. Gandásegui, et. al., *Las Luchas Obreras en Panamá: 1850-1978* (Panama City: CELA, 1980).

15. Sharon Phillipps, "Labor Policy in an Inclusionary-Authoritarian Regime: Panama Under Torrijos," Dissertation (University of New Mexico, July 1987), p. 79. Much of the information for this section on labor history is drawn from this study.

16. Gandásegui, *Las Luchas Obreras en Panamá*, op. cit., p. 43.

17. Hernando Franco Muñoz, *Movimiento Obrero Panameño 1914-1921* (Panama City: 1979), p. 15.

18. Phillipps, op. cit., p. 83.

19. Ibid., p. 86.

20. Renato Pereira, *Panamá: Fuerzas Armadas y Política* (Panama City: Ediciones Nueva Universidad, 1979), p. 22-23.

21. Carlos George, "La Conciliación y el Arbitraja en Materia Laboral y su Vigenica en Panamá," Thesis (Panama: Universidad de Panamá, 1972) p. 206, cited by Phillipps, op. cit., p. 88.

22. Walter LaFeber, *The Panama Canal: The Crisis in Historical Perspective* (New York: Oxford University Press, 1978), p. 171.

23. Jorge Fabrega, *Labor Code of the Republic of Panama* (Panama: Litho Impresora, 1974), cited in Phillipps, op. cit., p. 126.

24. There is some discussion whether Torrijos favored the more progressive CNTP over the CRTP. After the formation of the confederation in 1970, CNTP grew rapidly, counting on as many affiliates as the CRTP by the end of the decade. The 1973 CNTP National Congress was held in the National Assembly building, and the large banana unions both affiliated with the CNTP during the 1970s. But the CRTP was not shut out by the Torrijos regime. Its officials were appointed to head the Labor Ministry and as the country's ambassador to Jamaica.

25. David Dye, "The Good News is that Reagan's Gone, The Bad News is that Noriega Remains," *In These Times*, February 22, 1989.

26. Al Weinrub, "Panama's Unions Oppose U.S. Intervention," *Labor Report on Central America*, May-June 1988.

27. Victor Rodríguez, "La Coca-Cola de Panamá, *Diálogo Social,* June-July 1989.

28. AIFLD's Description of Operations in Panama for 1985, made available from AID's Latin American Regional Office.

29. Daphine Wysham, "Panama: Sovereignty Treaties," Distributed by CARNet, December 22, 1989.

30. U.S. Embassy, *Foreign Labor Trends: Panama* (Washington: Department of Labor, 1986).

31. The 1977 Panama Canal Treaties and their U.S. implementing legislation, Public Law 96-70 of 1979, established a special labor relations structure for U.S. military forces and the Panama Canal Commission which places all their civilian employees under U.S. federal labor law. U.S. Embassy, *Foreign Labor Trends*, op. cit., p. 10.

32. *Resumen Estadístico de UNESCO* (1987); Juan Bosco Bernal, "Estilos de Desarrollo, Educación, y Democracia," *Revista Panameña de Sociología,* VI Congreso Nacional de Sociología, 1989.

33. Caroline Aldrich-Langen and Kathleen Sellew, eds., *The Admission and Placement of Students from Central America,* A Projects for International Education Research (PIER) Report (Washington: National Association of Foreign Student Affairs, 1987), p. 208.

34. Juana Camargo, "Hacia Dónde Va la Educación," *Diálogo Social,* August 1988. In reference to national income, expenditures in education dropped from 5.5 percent in 1977 to 5.2 percent in 1986.

35. Aldrich-Langen and Sellew, *The Admission and Placement of Students,* op. cit., p. 215.

36. U.S. Information Service, *Panamanian Media 1968-1989.*

37. Roberto Fabrico, "Newspaperman Locked In Battle," *Miami Herald,* October 5, 1985. Eisenmann heads Eisenmann Enterprises, a large conglomerate of department stores and real estate, banking, and insurance firms.

38. The Duque family's Star and Herald Company also published a semi-independent English-language newspaper that ceased publication in October 1987 for economic (and some say political) reasons.

39. U.S. Information Service, *Panamanian Media 1968-1989.*

40. U.S. Embassy, "Country Data: Panama," January 1, 1989.

41. *Este País Mes a Mes,* April 1989, p. 5.

42. Arthur Golden, "La Prensa's Staff Faces Tough Times," *San Diego Union*, February 27, 1989; Fabrico, op. cit.
43. William Branigan, "U.S. Move in Panama Called Inept," *Washington Post*, April 29, 1989.
44. Ken Silverstein, "The Panama Story, or Here We Go Again," *Columbia Journalism Review*, May-June 1988, p. 20.
45. Otto S. Wald, "Condiciones Generales de Salud en la República de Panamá," *Revista Panameña de Sociología*, No. 3 (Universidad de Panamá, Departamento de Sociología, 1987); *Central America Report*, February 26, 1988.
46. Wald, op. cit.
47. Kenneth Jones, ed., *Panama Now* (Panama City: Focus Publications, 1986), p. 14.
48. *Central America Report*, September 29, 1989.
49. Paik-Swan Low, "Contraception: Is it Just Say No?" *Links* (NCAHRN), Winter 1987.
50. Amelia Plasencia, "Mala Nutrición en Panamá," *Diálogo Social*, October-November 1988.
51. Wald, op. cit.
52. World Health Organization, *World Health Statistics, Annual 1988*.
53. Ernesto A. and Carmelo Mesa-Lago, *La Seguridad Social en Panamá: Avances y Problemas*, cited in Wald, op. cit.
54. Clifton Holland, ed., *World Christianity, Volume 4: Central America and the Caribbean* (Monrovia, CA: Mission Advanced Research and Communication Center (MARC), World Vision International, 1981).
55. Betrand de la Grange, "Church Drops Neutral Facade," *Miami Herald*, May 21, 1989.
56. Holland, op. cit., p. 129. In the last decade, there has been an increase in native vocations, largely due to the expansion of the church from 23 parishes in the mid-1970s to 74 in the mid-1980s.
57. James C. Rauner, "The Church Suffers with the Poor," *America*, October 29, 1988.
58. For an excellent examination of the social and political role of the Catholic church see: Andrés Opazo Bernales, *Panamá: La Iglesia y la Lucha de los Pobres* (San José: DEI, 1988).
59. *Panama Now*, op. cit., p. 88.
60. Bernales, op. cit. p. 31.

61. Ibid., p. 48.

62. Ibid., p. 69.

63. Guillermo Meléndez, "Church Workers Unite Against Detractors," *Latinamerica Press*, June 16, 1983.

64. Clifton Holland, ed., *World Christianity, Volume 4: Central America and the Caribbean* (Monrovia, CA: Mission Advanced Research and Communication Center (MARC), World Vision International, 1981). This excellent overview of religion and churches was the source for most of this section on Protestantism in Panama.

65. Letter from Office of Development Affairs, March 23, 1988.

66. Cable to Department of State from U.S. Ambassador James Everett Briggs, "NED: Reported Use of Funds to Back Barletta," April 1984.

67. Interview by Debra Preusch with Domingo de Oladia of APEDE, March 28, 1989.

68. Interview by Debra Preusch with Victor Reina of YMCA, March 28, 1989.

69. Interview by Beth Sims with Larry Garber of National Democratic Institute for International Affairs, May 30, 1989.

70. Allen Weinstein, "U.S. Should Confess Failure in Panama," *Wall Street Journal*, May 9, 1989.

71. Interview be Debra Preusch with Gussie Daniels, Department of State, February 23, 1990.

72. "La Situación y Luchas de la Mujer en Panamá," *Cuadernos Liberación de la Mujer* (Partido Socialista de Trabajadores, ca. 1984). Women's right to vote was incorporated into the country's constitution in 1946.

73. Angela Alvarado, "La Desigualdad Jurídica de las Mujeres Panameñas," *Liberación*, May 1989. Also see: Andrés Bolaños Herrera, *La Discriminación de la Mujer en Panamá* (Panama City: n.p., 1987).

74. International Labor Office, *Panamá: Situación y Perspectivas del Empleo Femenino* (Santiago, Chile: OIT, 1984), Table 7, cited in International Center for Research on Women, "Integrating Women into Development Programs: A Guide for Implementation for Latin America and the Caribbean," *Gender Issues in Latin America and the Caribbean* (Washington: AID, May 1986), p. 10.

75. United Nations, *La Mujer en el Sector Urbano* (Santiago, Chile: UN, 1985).

76. *Cuadernos Liberación de la Mujer*, op. cit.

77. Urania Ungo, "La Mujer y La Cruzada Civilista," *Diálogo Social*, August-September 1987.

78. For a discussion of blacks and black organizing in Panama see: Gerardo Maloney, "El Movimiento Negro en Panamá," *Revista Panameña de Sociología*, No. 5 (Universidad de Panamá, Departamento de Sociología, 1989).

79. Michael L. Conniff, *Black Labor on a White Canal: Panama, 1904-1981* (Pittsburgh: University of Pittsburgh Press, 1985).

80. George Priestley, "Etnia, Clase, y Nación," *Tareas,* No. 67, October-December 1987, p. 39. Also see Conniff, op. cit.

81. Ibid., p. 40.

82. Ibid., p. 43. Arias was quickly deposed and the constitution annulled.

83. Ibid., p. 41.

84. Burton L. Gordon, *A Panama Forest and Shore: Natural History and Amerindian Culture in Bocas del Toro* (Boxwood Press, 1982).

85. "The History of the Guaymís: They Still Demand Their Land," *Barricada International*, February 25, 1988.

86. Gordon, op. cit.

87. The slash-and-burn agriculture requires a fallow period of 25 years — something no longer possible as the country's agricultural frontier shrinks.

88. For a fascinating examination of the workplace hazards facing the Guaymí migratory workforce see: Phillipe Bourgois, "Hazardous Pesticides in Panama: Guaymí Laborers at Risk," *Cultural Survival Quarterly*, Vol. 9(4), 1985.

89. Peter H. Herlihy, "Chocó Indian Relocation in Darién, Panama," *Cultural Survival Quarterly*, Vol. 9(2), pp. 43, 44.

90. Peter H. Herlihy, "Indians and Rainforest Collide: The Cultural Parks of Darién," *Cultural Survival Quarterly*, Vol. 10(3), pp. 57-61.

91. Gloria Evelyn Garvin, "Kuna Psychotherapeutics: A Psychological, Social, and Theoretical Analysis," (UMI Dissertation Service, degree date: 1983); James Howe, *The Kuna Gathering: Contemporary Village Politics in Panama* (Austin: University of Texas Press, 1986), p. 9.

92. Howe, op. cit., pp. 10-13.

93. Brian Houseal, Craig MacFarland, Guillermo Archibold, and Aurelio Chiari, "Indigenous Cultures and Protected Areas in

Central America," *Cultural Survival Quarterly*, Vol. 9(1), 1985, pp. 15-18.

94. Howe, op. cit., pp. 24-28.

95. Ibid.

96. Jason Clay, "Indigenous People and Tropical Forests: Models of Land Use and Management from Latin America," *Cultural Survival Report 27*, 1988, pp. 66-67.

97. U.S. Government Accounting Office, "Central America: Conditions of Refugees and Displaced Persons," March 1989.

98. H. Jeffrey Leonard, *Natural Resources and Economic Development in Central America* (New Brunswick, NJ: Transaction Books, 1987), pp. 26, 27.

99. Ibid., p. 25; "Global Status of Mangrove Ecosystems," *Environmentalist*, Supplement 3, 1983.

100. Leonard, op. cit., p. 156.

101. Ibid., p. 18.

102. *Panama Now*, op. cit., p. 97.

103. Leonard, op. cit., pp. 130, 131.

104. *The Amicus Journal*, Fall 1988.

105. Panama Canal Commission, "Reports to Congress, 1986."

106. *Ancon Boletín*, January 1989.

107. "Falsos Ecologistas No Son Otra Cosa Que Políticos Voraces," *Crítica*, November 24, 1988.

108. Gloria Batista, "The Campaign to Save the Atlantic Coast of Panama," *Earth Island Journal*, Winter 1988.

Chapter Five

1. Diane de Graffenreid, ed., *Panama: Sovereignty for a Land Divided* (Washington: EPICA Task Force, 1976), p. 11.

2. Richard F. Nyrop, ed., *Panama: A Country Study* (Washington: American University, 1981), p.198.

3. *NACLA Report on the Americas*, September-October 1979, p.13.

4. Ibid., p.3.

5. For a thorough examination of U.S.-Panama relations see: Walter LaFeber, *The Panama Canal: The Crisis in Historical Perspective* (New York: Oxford University Press, 1979).

6. Nyrop, op. cit., p.166.

7. *NACLA Report on the Americas*, September-October 1979, op. cit., p.4.

8. Ibid.

9. Opposition to the 1977 Canal Treaties were instrumental in forging the New Right in the 1970s. Among its principal strategists were Paul Weyrich of the Free Congress Research and Education Foundation, Howard Phillips of the Conservative Caucus, the late Terry Nolan who founded the National Conservative Political Action Committee, and Dick Viguerie, the New Right's direct mail expert. James Ridgeway, "The Canal Is Ours," *Village Voice*, June 14, 1988.

10. Thomas John Bossert, "Panama," in Morris Blachman and William LeoGrande, eds., *Inside Central America: The Impact of U.S. Policy* (New York: Pantheon, 1987), p. 202.

11. Ibid., p. 203.

12. For good accounts of the U.S.-Noriega relationship see: John Dinges, *Our Man in Panama* (New York: Random House, 1990), and Frederick Kempe, *Divorcing the Dictator* (New York: G.P. Putnam's Sons, 1990).

13. Frederick Kempe, "U.S. Taught Noriega to Spy, But Pupil Bested His Teachers," *Wall Street Journal*, October 18, 1989. Much of the information in this section on Noriega's relationship with the U.S. government comes from this revealing article.

14. Kempe, *Divorcing the Dictator*, op. cit.

15. Seymour M. Hersh, "U.S. Aides in '72 Weighed Killing Officer Who Now Leads Panama," *New York Times*, June 13, 1986.

16. John Weeks and Andrew Zimbalist, "The Failure of Intervention in Panama," *Third World Quarterly*, January 1989, pp. 8-9; *New York Times Magazine*, May 19, 1988; Seymour Hersh, "Panama Strongman Said to Trade in Drugs, Arms, and Illicit Money," *New York Times*, June 12, 1986.

17. This split is discussed in John Weeks, "Panama: Current Political Instability," *Third World Quarterly*, July 1987, p. 787.

18. Richard Millet, "Looking Beyond Noriega," *Foreign Policy*, Summer 1988, p. 47.

19. *Washington Report on the Hemisphere*, January 24, 1990.

20. Rober Burbach, "Panamanian Addendum," *Strategic Perspectives*, January 1990.

21. Information from Major Kathy Wood, Department of Defense Public Affairs, February 23, 1989.

22. *Panorama Católico*, January 14, 1990.

23. Dinges, op. cit; Michael Isikoff, "Analysts Challenge View of Noriega as Drug Lord," *The Washington Post*, January 7, 1990.

24. President Endara is a close friend of Carlos Eleta and was the attorney for several companies owned by Eleta, a political opposition figure arrested in April 1989 on the suspicion of smuggling hundreds of pounds of cocaine into the United States. Endara has for years been the director of Banco Oceánico, one of two dozen banks in Panama named by the FBI as laundering drug money. The new Labor Minister, Jorge Rubén Rosas, was Eleta's trial attorney. Vice President Guillermo Ford is part owner of the Dadeland Bank of Florida, which has received deposits from the Medellín Cartel. Attorney General Rogelio Cruz, Chief Justice Carlos López, and Treasury Minister Mario Galindo all sat on the board of the Inter-Americas Bank, which was shut down in 1985 by Washington after its ownership by a leader of the Cali Cartel was established. *New York Times*, February 6, 1990; *Washington Report on the Hemisphere*, February 21, 1990.

25. *Panama: Sovereignty for a Land Divided*, op. cit., p. 11.

26. *Latin American Weekly Report*, March 2, 1989.

27. U.S. Embassy, *Investment Climate Survey* (Washington: U.S. Chamber of Commerce, February 2, 1988); Department of Commerce, *Survey of Current Business*, June 1988.

28. Charlotte Elton, "Serving Foreigners," *NACLA Report on the Americas*, July-August 1988.

29. U.S. Embassy, "Business Facts Sheets: Panama," October 1988.

30. Millet, op. cit., p.58.

31. These included Lake Resources, Udall Research Corporation, and Human Development Foundation.

32. According to U.S. embassy figures, U.S. productive investment in Panama as of 1987 was in the following sectors: petroleum and pipeline, $750 million; agriculture and seafood, $330 million; banking, $200 million; commerce and medical care, $85 million; other manufacturing, $40 million; chemicals and pharmaceuticals, $35 million; food processing, $20 million; insurance and financial services, $20 million; shipping, communications, and transport, $15 million; and tourism, $5 million. U.S. Embassy, *Investment Climate Survey*, op. cit. According to the U.S. embassy, the major U.S. firms

doing business in Panama include: Agro Marina, Alcoa Interamericana, Armour Company, Arthur Young and Co., Arthur Anderson, Black and Decker, Borden, Bristol Laboratory, Burroughs, Chiriquí Land Company (United Brands),Chrysler, Colgate-Palmolive, Coopers & Lybrand, Deloitte Haskins & Sells, Del Monte, Eastern Airlines, Ernst & Whitney, Esso Standard Oil, Firestone, Ford, General Mills, Gillette, Goodyear, IBM, Jenny Manufacturing, Johnson & Johnson, Kativo, Kimberly-Clark, Kodak, Nabisco Brands, NCR, Peat, Marwick, Mitchell, Phillip Morris, Price Waterhouse, Schering, Sherwin Williams, Texaco, Touche Ross, and Wang, as well as the following banks: Citibank, Chase Manhattan, Bank of America, Marine Midland, American Express Bank, Merrill Lynch International Bank, Republic National Bank, Philadelphia National Bank, and Bank of Boston. U.S. Embassy, *Investment Climate Survey*, op. cit.

33. Data from the Resource Center Compilation of Corporations, 1985; Tom Barry and Debra Preusch, *The Central America Fact Book* (New York: Grove Press, 1986), p. 310.

34. "U.S. Transnationals Profit During Regional Crisis," *Central America Report*, December 11, 1987, citing data from the Department of Commerce.

35. Elton, "Serving Foreigners," op. cit.

36. William Branigin, "U.S. Firms Seek Change in Panama Sanctions," *New York Times*, April 4, 1989.

37. Peter Kennedy, "Latest Round of U.S. Sanctions Against Panama's Regime May Send U.S. Firms Packing," *Business Latin America*, September 25, 1989.

38. Agency for International Development, *Country Development Strategy Statement: Panama 1984* (Washington: January 1982).

39. Agency for International Development, *Country Development Strategy Statement: Panama FY1988-1992* (Washington: February 1986), p. 33.

40. Agency for International Development, *Congressional Presentation, FY 1988, Annex III* (Washington: 1987), p. 165.

41. Ibid., p. 164.

42. H. Jeffrey Leonard, *Natural Resources and Economic Development in Central America* (New Brunswick, NJ: Transaction Books, 1987), pp. 113-137.

43. White House, "Statement by the President," January 25, 1990.

44. Agency for International Development, "Panama Immediate Recovery Program," February 1990.

45. See special issue of *Military Review* (February 1989) on "U.S. SOUTHCOM: High-Probability Conflict" for the latest U.S. military thinking on the role of the Southern Command in low-intensity conflict. Also see Michael Klare, "Panama Signals New U.S. Military Mission in Third World," *Pacific News Service*, December 21, 1989.

46. Alfonso Chardy, "U.S. May Close Bases," *Miami Herald*, May 7, 1989.

47. SOUTHCOM covers 22 percent of the territories assigned to the four regional commands but only counts for 0.1 percent of the Pentagon's budget and 0.5 percent of its military personnel.

48. U.S. SOUTHCOM, "Information Sheet," January 1989.

49. Information for this section on SOUTHCOM comes largely from SOUTHCOM's *Information Booklet* compiled by the U.S. SOUTHCOM Public Affairs Office, January 1989. Also see: Raúl Leis, *Comando Sur: Poder Hostil* (Panama City: CEASPA, 1985).

50. U.S. Government Accounting Office, *Security Assistance: Update of Programs and Related Assistance* (Washington: December 1988. Worth noting is that U.S. commercial military sales continued even after the June 1987 cutoff of U.S. military aid. These sales decreased in 1987 but rose to an unprecedented $8 million in 1988.

51. *Central America Report*, May 12, 1989.

52. Ibid.; *Latin American Weekly Report*, January 5, 1989; Chardy, op. cit.

53. Estación Sismología e Instituto de Geociencia, "Reporte Especial de Actividad del Día 20 de Diciembre," *Este País Mes a Mes*, February 1990.

54. Raúl Leis, "Diez Ideas sobre el Panamá de Hoy," *Este País Mes a Mes*, February 1990.

55. Press reports cited by Noam Chomsky in "Post Cold War Cold War," *Z Magazine*, March 1990.

56. Ken Stier, "Panama Charm Fades," *Far Eastern Economic Review*, June 15, 1989.

57. Ibid.

58. Allan Dodds Frank, "Everyone Wants Us," *Forbes*, February 23, 1987.

59. Stier, op. cit.

60. Charlotte Elton, *El Canal de Panamá y Los Intereses Japoneses en América Latina* (Panama City: CEASPA, September 1987), p. 14.

61. *Journal of Commerce*, May 2, 1989.

62. Joel Millman, "Central America is Fertile Ground for Taiwan's Surplus," *Wall Street Journal*, July 1, 1988.

63. Augusto Varas, *Soviet-Latin American Relations in the 1980s* (Boulder: Westview Press, 1987), p. 74.

64. See *Israeli Foreign Affairs*, May 1987, and March, April, May, June, July, August, October 1988, and October and November 1989.

65. *San Francisco Examiner*, October 22, 1989, as cited in *Israeli Foreign Affairs*, November 1989.

66. *San Francisco Examiner*, October 22, 1989 and *Houston Chronicle*, October 18, 1989, as cited in *Israeli Foreign Affairs*, November 1989.

67. *Israeli Foreign Affairs*, November 1989.

68. *Israeli Foreign Affairs*, February 1990.

Statistics

Population

Population:	2,322,000 (1988)[1]
Urban Population:	50.6% (1988)[1]
Population Density:	79.5 per sq. mi. (1988)[1]
Annual Growth Rate:	2.2% (1980-1988)[1]
Literacy:	85.8% (1986)[1]

Ethnic Composition:[2]

Mestizo	70%
Antillean Negro	14%
White	9%
Indian	7%

Religion (1981):[3]

Catholic:	86%
Protestant:	12%

Health

Life Expectancy at Birth:	71 years (1980-1985)[1]
Infant Mortality per 1,000 Live Births:	22.7 (1986)[1]

Economy

GDP:	$5,797 million (1987)[1]
Per Capita GDP:	$2,549 (1987)[1]

Per Capita GDP Growth Rate:[1]

1961-1980:	3.7%
1981-1985:	0.6%

Gross Domestic Investment:[1]

1961-1970:	13.4%
1971-1980:	3.8%
1981-1988:	-3.8%

Income Distribution (1980):[4]

Poorest 22% of Population:	5.5%
Richest 15%:	55.4%

External Public Debt:

1970:	$194 million[5]
1988:	$4170 million[6]

Trade Balance:	-$450 million (1989)[7]
Debt Servicing as % of Exports:	84.0%[4]
External Debt as % of GNP:	70.2%[4]
Income & Property Taxes as % of Current Revenues:	38.5% (1988)[1]
Labor Force by Sector (1986):[8]	
Agriculture:	28.6%
Government & Community Services:	28.4%
Commerce:	14.6%
Unemployment:	21% (1988)[9]
Underemployment:	9.7% (1986)[8]
Real Minimum Wage as Compared to 1980 Wages:[1]	
1970:	119.3%
1985:	100.9%
Top Agricultural Products as % of Total Exports:	
Bananas (1983-1987):	23.3%[1]
Shrimp (1987):	21%[10]
Sugar (1983-1987):	8.5%[1]

U.S. Economic Aid[11]
(millions of dollars)

	1946-1979	1980-1987	1988	1989	1990*
Development Assistance	279.6	70.4	1.1	0	0
ESF	28.2	62.0	0	0	530.1
PL480	20.9	6.8	0	0.3	15.0
Peace Corps	6.9	0	0	0	0
Total	335.6	139.2	1.1	0.3	545.1

U.S. Military Aid[11]
(millions of dollars)

	1946-1979	1980-1987	1988	1989	1990*
MAP	4.7	24.8	0	0	0
FMS	3.5	18.8	0	0	9.0
IMET	4.8	3.7	0	0	0
Total	13.0	47.3	0	0	9.0

*Requested

Sources:
1) Economic and Social Progress in Latin America: 1989 Report, Inter-American Development Bank; 2) Encyclopedia of the Third World, 1987; 3) World Christianity, Volume 4: Central America and the Caribbean, Missions and Advanced Research and Communication (MARC), a division of World Vision International, 1981; 4) Centro de Estudios y Acción Social Panameño (CEASPA), February 1990; 5) World Development Report 1988, World Bank; 6) Notas sobre la Economía y el Desarrollo, CEPAL, December 1988; 7) Miami Herald, "Hemisphere '89," April 17, 1989; 8) Foreign Economic Trends, U.S.

Department of Commerce, March 1988; 9) Business Latin America, January 16, 1989; 10) Europa Yearbook 1988; 11) U.S. Overseas Loans and Grants: Obligations and Loan Authorizations July 1, 1945-September 30, 1983, Agency for International Development, Office of Planning and Budgeting; U.S. Overseas Loans and Grants: Obligations and Loan Authorizations July 1, 1945-September 30, 1987, Agency for International Development, Office of Planning and Budgeting; Fiscal Year 1990 Summary Tables, Agency for International Development; White House, Fact Sheet, "Partnership with Panama: Action Plan to Foster Economic Recovery," January 1990.

Chronology

1534   King Charles V of Spain orders the territorial governor to study the possibility of building a canal to join the Chagres River and the South Sea.

1694   William Patterson, founder of the Bank of England, tries to interest the English king in a canal through the Isthmus of Panama.

1789   Alexander Von Humbolt explores America and recommends nine possible routes for an interoceanic canal; among them are: Nicaragua, Panama, and the Valley of the Atrato River in what is now Colombia.

1821   Panama declares independence from Spain and becomes a province of Great Colombia.

1834   The Congress of New Granada authorizes the construction of a canal, railroad, or road through the Isthmus of Panama.

1840   Revolt gives Panama brief independence until 1842.

1846   U.S.-New Grenada treaty; United States guarantees neutrality and the sovereign rights of New Granada on the Isthmus.

1849   Gold rush makes Panama a valuable transit route from the U.S. east coast to California.

1850   U.S. businessmen finance construction of 48-mile Panama Railway, completed in 1855.

1856   U.S. troops protect the trans-isthmian railroad from possible attacks by Panamanian independence forces for next nine years.

1863   New Grenada renamed Colombia.

1865   U.S. troops intervene three times in the next eight years to protect U.S. interests.

1878   French Panama Canal Company acquires exclusive right to build canal through Panama.

1882   Canal construction companies have financial problems for next decade.

1899   Civil war breaks out in Colombia.

1902   U.S. Congress authorizes the president to acquire from Colombia a strip of land in Panama to build an interoceanic canal.

1903   Secessionists declare the Department of Panama an independent republic; the new flag is raised by a member of the U.S. Army Corps of Engineers as three U.S. gunboats prevent the landing of Colombian troops.

Secretary of State John Hay and French entrepreneur Philippe Bunau Varilla formulate a canal treaty very favorable to the United States. The Hay-Bunau Varilla Treaty between United States and Panama is signed, authorizing the United States to construct, maintain, operate, protect, and sanitize an interoceanic canal through Panama "in perpetuity," and allowing the United

States to act in the Canal Zone "as if it were the sovereign of the territory." The Panamanian signatory lacked the full powers and credentials to sign the treaty.

1904   U.S. troops intervene to quash protests against the Hay-Bunau Varilla Treaty.

New constitution promulgated which grants the United States the right to intervene "in any part of Panama, to reestablish public peace and constitutional order." Panama informs the United States that the canal treaty does not entail a territorial grant or transfer of sovereignty.

National army disbanded and Panama establishes monetary system based on U.S. dollar.

The governor of the Canal Zone, on instructions from the U.S. president, opens the Zone to international trade, and establishes duties on imported goods.

1908   U.S. troops intervene in Panama for first of four times within the next decade.

National elections held under U.S. supervision.

1914   Panama Canal opens for operation.

1918   Constitutional crisis; U.S. troops intervene in Panama City and Colón during elections; liberal Porras installed as president.

U.S. troops intervene in the Chiriquí province and remain for next two years to protect United Fruit Company plantations.

1920   United Brotherhood of Maintenance Way calls a strike of over 17,000 canal workers.

1921   U.S. troops intervene in border conflicts between Panama and Costa Rica.

Formation of the Workers Federation of the Republic of Panama.

1925   A rent strike prompts the arrival of U.S. troops in Panama City.

1926   Panama and United States sign a treaty designed to eliminate conflicts, but which legalizes many of them. Treaty is rejected by Panamanian Assembly.

1930   Government curtails labor organizing for next 15 years.

1932   Election of Harmodio Arias Madrid.

1936   Election of J. D. Arosemana.

Panama and United States sign the General Treaty of Friendship and Cooperation, which maintains all stipulations of 1903 treaty except the guarantee of Panama's independence and right of the United States to intervene in Panama.

1939   Revised treaty ratified.

Arosemana dies and is replaced by First Vice President Boyd.

1940   National Party candidate Arnulfo Arias Madrid elected.

1941   New constitution promulgated.

Adolfo de la Guardia replaces Arias in coup.

1942   Treaty with United States to allow U.S. stations and airfields on Panamanian territory; treaty is to expire in six years. Many U.S. military bases built upon the entry of the United States into World War II.

1945   National Assembly refuses to grant de la Guardia an extension of his term.

Reemergence of labor movement.

Formation of the Trade Union Federation of the Republic of Panama.

1946   New constitution promulgated; Enrique Jiménez elected as provisional president.

The U.S. Army opens the School of the Americas ("the school of coups") in violation of the 1903 treaty which only allows for the presence of U.S. troops for defense of the canal.

1947   New treaty on U.S. military sites is rejected by the National Assembly after popular pressure.

1948   Constitutional crisis; National Assembly dismisses Jiménez and elects Enrique Obarrio.

Díaz Arosemana defeats Arias in national presidential elections.

Colón Free Trade Zone created in Panama based on a proposal by a New York banker.

1949   Death of Díaz Arosemana; succession by First Vice President Daniel Chanis, who attempts to dismiss National Guard Commander José Antonio Remón Cantera, but is ousted himself. Remón installs Arias.

1951   Arias ousted; formation of a coalition government led by Alcibiades Arosemana.

1952   National Patriotic Coalition candidate Remón elected president.

1953   United States creates the Panamanian National Guard modeled after Anastasio Somoza's Nicaraguan National Guard. In the coming years, National Guard officers are trained in Nicaragua, Peru, and at the U.S. Army School of the Americas.

1955   Remón assassinated; First Vice President José Guizado inaugurated and then impeached due to suspicion of his involvement in Remón's death; Second Vice President Ricardo Arias Espinoza installed as president.

1956   Treaty of Mutual Understanding and Cooperation (Remón-Eisenhower Treaty) is signed.

National Patriotic Coalition candidate Ernesto de la Guardia elected.

Formation of the Confederation of Workers of the Republic of Panama with U.S. prompting and Panamanian government support.

1958   University students plant Panamanian flags in the Canal Zone under "Operation Sovereignty."

1959   Anti-U.S. demonstrations over sovereignty of the Canal Zone; Hunger and Desperation March sparks new renters' law and minimum wage.

1960   National Opposition Union candidate Roberto Chiari elected.

Panama Canal Zone becomes a center for U.S.-sponsored counterinsurgency training.

1962   Presidents Chiari and Kennedy agree to designate negotiators to review the 1903 treaty; also agree to display the Panamanian flag in the Canal Zone.

1963   A joint Panamanian-U.S. statement advising that the Panamanian flag be flown along side the U.S. flag in the Canal Zone.

1964

Jan.   Students attempting to fly the Panamanian flag next to the U.S. flag at a high school are attacked by Canal Zone residents. During subsequent Flag Riots, 28 people are killed, more than 300 wounded, and over 500 arrested; diplomatic relations with United States severed; OAS called in to mediate.

Apr.   Diplomatic relations with United States restored; negotiations begin to draft new treaties to resolve the conflicts.

June   Study groups from the University of Panama and the National Bar Association object to the draft treaties.

Marco Aurelio Robles elected president.

1968   Constitutional crisis; Arnulfo Arias Madrid elected again but is deposed within ten days of being sworn in. Junta is formed, but power is assumed by

Commander in Chief of the Defense Forces Col. Omar Torrijos Herrera after he overthrows the coup's leader, Boris Martínez.

1969   Abortive coup attempt against Torrijos; he instead consolidates power.

1970   Panama advises the United States that the draft treaties do not eliminate the causes of conflict, and that Panama is ready to continue searching for a solution.

Panamanian government assumes control of the U.S. military base of Río Hato after refusing to renew provisions of the 1955 treaty.

1972   Election of a National Assembly of Community Representatives.

New constitution promulgated; Torrijos named "Supreme Leader of the Panamanian Revolution" with virtually unlimited powers.

New Labor Code becomes effective.

1973   United Nations Security Council meets in Panama and prepares a resolution exhorting Panama and the United States to continue negotiations to arrive at a treaty returning the Canal Zone to Panama. The United States vetoes the resolution.

1974   Panama and United States agree to begin new negotiations.

1976   New labor law negates many benefits of the 1972 Code.

1977   Presidents Torrijos and Carter sign the Panama Canal Treaties in Washington D.C. giving Panama control of the canal at noon on December 31, 1999. The accords replace the U.S. government agency Panama Canal Co. with a jointly supervised Panama Canal Commission. A Panamanian is to take office as administrator of the Commission on January 1, 1990. The canal treaties are approved in Panama.

Comunbana becomes marketing arm of UPEB. United Brands refuses to load Comunbana ships in Panama, government threatens nationalization of United Brands acreage.

1978   Canal treaties ratified by U.S. Senate with the provision that permits U.S. intervention if the canal's operation is interrupted, though such action shall not be interpreted as a right of intervention in Panama's sovereignty or internal affairs.

National Assembly elects Aristides Royo president.

Formation of Revolutionary Democratic Party (PRD).

1979   Panama canal treaties go into effect and U.S. control of the Canal Zone officially ends.

Arrival of the deposed Shah of Iran, triggering demonstrations and protests.

1981   Torrijos dies in an unexplained plane crash; Col. Florencio Flores succeeds him as head of the National Guard.

1982   President Royo resigns under pressure from National Guard; Ricardo De La Espriella becomes president.

Rubén Darío Paredes ousts Flores as head of National Guard.

1983   National Guard renamed Panama Defense Forces (PDF); police forces are separated from military forces but under PDF control. Paredes resigns and briefly enters his candidacy for president.

Gen. Manuel Antonio Noriega, CIA asset trained at the School of the Americas and head of military intelligence, becomes commander of the Panama Defense Forces.

Jan.   The Contadora Group, composed of Colombia, Mexico, Panama, and Venezuela, meets for the first time on the Panamanian island of Contadora to develop

	peace accords to which Costa Rica, El Salvador, Guatemala, Honduras, and Nicaragua are parties.
Sep.	Contadora peace plan unveiled which calls for a policy of nonaggression in the Caribbean Basin.
Oct.	The United States invades Grenada.

1984

Jan.	A student immolates himself in front of the U.S. embassy.
Feb.	President De La Espriella resigns and is replaced by Jorge Illueca Sibuaste.
May	PRD candidate Nicolás Ardito Barletta narrowly defeats Arnulfo Arias Madrid in fraudulent elections.
Sep.	School of the Americas closes after training nearly 45,000 Latin American officers; it relocates in Ft. Benning, Georgia, four months later.
Oct.	New government inaugurated. Secretary of State George Shultz attends the inauguration ceremony and calls Ardito Barletta "a longtime and respected friend."

1985	Dr. Hugo Spadafora, a former vice minister of health, is assassinated upon his return from a visit to Costa Rica.
Sep.	The military is accused of complicity in the assassination of Spadafora; Ardito Barletta resigns; Noriega installs industrialist Erick Arturo Delvalle. The Reagan administration shows its displeasure by canceling a display of aerobatics by the U.S. Air Force Thunderbirds.
Dec.	Admiral John Poindexter travels to Panama to confer with Noriega.

1986

Jan.	Blazing Trail and Kindle Liberty U.S. joint exercises in Honduras and Panama begin and continue for six months.
June	U.S. newspapers allege that Noriega trafficks in drugs and supplies arms to Colombian guerrillas.
	Oliver North plans to frame the Sandinistas by "capturing" a ship with eastern bloc arms in the canal; plan fails when Noriega seizes the ship and exposes the scheme.

1987

June	An ousted second-in-command of the Defense Forces accuses Noriega of rigging the 1984 elections and murdering Dr. Hugo Spadafora; anti-government rioting results; ten-day "state of urgency" declared; constitutional guarantees suspended.
	Panamanian government informs the United States and other creditor nations that it is stopping all principal and interest payments. Rumors of printing Panamanian currency leads to heavy bank withdrawals.
	U.S. Senate calls for Noriega to step down and calls for new elections. U.S. embassy attacked by a hundred protesters; United States demands payment for damages to building.
Sep.	Secretary of State George Shultz formally approves freeze of U.S. economic and military aid to Panama.
Dec.	All U.S. military and economic aid suspended; sugar quota suspended.
	Panamanian government fails to pay Christmas bonuses to government employees.

1988

Feb.   U.S. Justice Department seals indictments charging Noriega and others with international drug trafficking.

After a meeting with Elliott Abrams, President Delvalle attempts to fire Noriega. But Delvalle is himself ousted by the National Assembly, which then appoints Manuel Solís Palma. Delvalle goes into hiding but is recognized by the United States as Panama's president.

Run begins on national banks by depositors, and strikes by opposition occur.

Mar.   U.S. government freezes Panama's assets abroad and Delvalle urges a boycott of the country.

Government closes the nation's banks, which remain closed for nine weeks.

U.S. government withholds payments of the Panama Canal Commission and suspends trade preferences for Panama.

Coup attempt shuts down economy; massive power outages shut down trans-isthmian oil pipeline; transportation disrupted; two-week general strike.

Dignity battalions are formed and begin training to fight against a possible U.S. invasion.

Apr.   President Reagan bars U.S. companies and individuals from making payments to the Panamanian government, instead asking them to make payments to the Delvalle-controlled federal reserve account.

May   Secret bargaining collapses between Reagan administration and Noriega.

July   CIA develops a coup plan which might result in Noriega's assassination by dissident officers; plan nixed by Senate Select Committee on Intelligence and opposition is given a mobile transmitter instead.

Aug.   United States charges more than 240 cases of harassment against U.S. military personnel by Panamanian authorities.

1989

May   ADOC candidate Guillermo Endara apparently wins presidential election; election nullified by Noriega regime.

President Bush recalls U.S. ambassador, dispatches an additional 2,000 troops to Panama, and tells Pentagon to stage a series of aggressive maneuvers.

OAS forms a mediation commission with the foreign ministers of Ecuador, Guatemala, and Trinidad-Tobago.

July   OAS ministers propose that Noriega step down, a government of transition take power, and elections be held at a later date; they also call for an end to U.S. military and economic aggression, compliance with 1977 Canal Treaties, and OAS mediation during the negotiation process.

Estimated 75,000 civil servants protest U.S. army maneuvers along the canal banks.

The U.S. commander in Panama, critical of Bush's escalating policies, is replaced by the aggressive Gen. Maxwell R. Thurman who is told to prepare for an invasion.

Aug.   Panama calls for an urgent meeting of the UN Security Council because of the U.S. maneuvers.

United States rejects calls from the OAS to lift sanctions and presents alleged proof of Noriega's involvement in drug trafficking.

Sep.   General Council of State names provisional government led by Francisco Rodríguez and announces elections will be called within six months after sanctions are lifted. United States withdraws its ambassador; many Latin American ambassadors called home for consultations.

Oct.   Failed coup attempt against Noriega.
Nov.   Bush administration bans Panamanian flagged ships from U.S. ports.
Dec.   Noriega elected head of government with unlimited powers by National
         Assembly.

         U.S. invasion with 26,000 troops; United States installs Endara as president; after
         two weeks in hiding and sanctuary in the Vatican embassy, Noriega turns
         himself over to U.S. officials.
1990   Noriega arraigned in Miami on drug charges.

Sources for the chronology include: The Central America Fact Book by Tom Barry and Debra Preusch (Grove Press, 1986); Conflict in Central America (United Kingdom: Longman Group Limited, 1987); U.S. Embassy in Panama (1975); Encyclopedia of the Third World (1987); Labor Organizations in Latin America, Gerald Greenfield and Sheldon Maran, eds. (Greenwood Press, 1987); The Washington Post (May 10, 1989); The Nation (March 12, 1988); Brecha, CODEHUCA (May-June 1989); Central America Education Project (Summer 1987); Regionews from Managua, Pensamiento Propio, September 1989; Albuquerque Journal (October 4, 1989); The Nation (March 12, 1988).

Bibliography

The following periodicals are useful sources of information and analysis on Panama:

Central America Bulletin, Central America Research Institute, monthly, English.

Diálogo Social, Centro de Capacitación Social (Panama), monthly, Spanish.

Este País Mes a Mes, Centro de Estudios y Acción Social Panameño (Panama), monthly, Spanish.

NACLA Report on the Americas, North American Congress on Latin America, bi-monthly, English.

Pensamiento Propio, Coordinadora Regional de Investigaciones Económicas y Sociales (Managua), monthly, Spanish.

Tareas, Revista del Centro de Estudios Latinoamericanos (Panama), bi-monthly, Spanish.

The following reports and books contain valuable background on many issues important to understanding Panama:

Congreso Nacional de Sociología, *Revista Panameña de Sociología* (Panama: Imprenta Universitaria, 1989).

Michael L. Conniff, *Black Labor on a White Canal: Panama, 1904-1981* (Pittsburgh: University of Pittsburgh Press, 1985).

John Dinges, *Our Man in Panama* (New York: Random House, 1990).

Marco A. Gandásegui, hijo, *Panamá: Crisis Política y Agresión Económica* (Panama: Centro de Estudios Latinoamericanos, 1989).

Simeón González H., *La Crisis del Torrijismo y las Elecciones de 1984* (Panama: Ediciones Horizonte, 1985).

Diane de Graffenreid, ed., *Panama: Sovereignty for a Land Divided* (Washington: EPICA Task Force, 1976).

William R. Hughes and Ivan A. Quintero, *¿Quiénes Son los Dueños de Panamá?* (Panama: Centro de Estudios y Acción Social Panameño, 1987).

Inforpress Centroamericana, *Centro América 1988: Análisis Económicos y Políticos Sobre la Región* (Guatemala: Inforpress Centroamericana, 1988).

Kenneth Jones, ed., *Panama Now* (Panama City: Focus Publications, 1986).

Frederick Kempe, *Divorcing the Dictator* (New York: G.P. Putnam's Sons, 1990).

Walter LaFeber, *The Panama Canal: The Crisis in Historical Perspective* (New York: Oxford University Press, 1978).

Andrés Opazo Bernales, *Panama: La Iglesia y la Lucha de los Pobres* (San José: Departamento Ecuménico de Investigaciones, 1988).

Sharon Phillipps, *Labor Policy in an Inclusionary-Authoritarian Regime: Panama Under Torrijos*, Dissertation (Albuquerque: University of New Mexico, 1987).

Nestor Porcell, *El Panameño Actual y Otros Ensayos* (Panama: Universidad de Panama, 1986).

George Priestley, *Military Government and Popular Participation in Panama: The Torrijos Regime, 1968-1975* (Boulder: Westview Press, 1986).

U.S. Agency for International Development, *Panama: Country Development Strategy Statement FY 1988-1992* (Washington: AID, 1986).

U.S. Military Southern Command, *Information Booklet* (Quarry Heights: U.S. SOUTHCOM Public Affairs Office, 1989).

The World Bank, *Panama: Structural Change and Growth Prospects* (Washington: World Bank, 1985).

For More Information

Resources

Centro de Capacitación Social (CCS) / Diálogo Social
Apartado Postal 9A-192
Panamá, República de Panamá

Centro de Estudios y Acción Social Panameño (CEASPA) /
Este País Mes a Mes, Momento Centroamericano
Apartado Postal 6-133, El Dorado
Panamá, República de Panamá

Centro de Estudios Latinoamericanos Justo Arosemana (CELA) / Tareas
Apartado Postal 6-3093, El Dorado
Panamá, República de Panamá

Instituto de Estudios Nacionales (IDEN)
Universidad de Panamá
Estafeta Universitaria
Panamá, República de Panamá

Human Rights

Americas Watch
1522 K Street NW, Suite 910
Washington DC 20005

Amnesty International
322 8th Avenue
New York, NY 10001

Coordinadora Popular de Derechos Humanos en Panamá (COPODEHUPA)
Apartado Postal 1151, Zona 1
Panamá, República de Panamá

Official

Embassy of Panama
2862 McGill Terrace NW
Washington DC 20008-2748

Embassy of the United States in Panama
APO Miami, FL 34002

U.S. State Department
Citizen's Emergency Center/Travel Information
Main State Building
Washington DC 20520
(202) 647-5225